I.L.L.

26/05/06

University of Plymouth Library

Subject to status this item may be renewed
via your Voyager account

http://voyager.plymouth.ac.uk

Exeter tel: (01392) 475049
Exmouth tel: (01395) 255331
Plymouth tel: (01752) 232323

THE TYRANNY OF HATE
THE ROOTS OF ANTISEMITISM

A Translation into English of
Memsheleth Sadon

Constantin Brunner

1862-1937

THE TYRANNY OF HATE
THE ROOTS OF ANTISEMITISM

A Translation into English of
Memsheleth Sadon
by
Constantin Brunner

Translated by
Graham Harrison

Abridged and Edited by
Aron M. Rappaport

The Edwin Mellen Press
Lewiston/Queenston/Lampeter

Library of Congress Cataloging-in-Publication Data

Brunner, Constantin, 1862-1937.
    [Memscheleth sadon. English]
    Tyranny of hate : the roots of antisemitism : a translation of
Memsheleth sadon / by Constantin Brunner ; translated by Graham
Harrison ; abridged and edited by Aron M. Rappaport.
        p.   cm.
    Includes bibliographical references and index.
    ISBN 0-7734-9562-2
    1. Antisemitism--Psychological aspects. 2. Jews--Politics and
government. 3. Hate. I. Rappaport, Aron M. II. Title.
DS145.B7613   1992
305.8'92'4--dc20   92-13724
                                                                         CIP

A CIP catalog record for this book
is available from the British Library.

The Edwin Mellen Press   The Edwin Mellen Press
        Box 450   Box 67
Lewiston, New York   Queenston, Ontario
     USA 14092   CANADA L0S 1L0

The Edwin Mellen Press, Ltd.
Lampeter, Dyfed, Wales
UNITED KINGDOM SA48 7DY

Printed in the United States of America

In memory

of

Samuel Aba and Henriette Rappaport

victims of the holocaust,

and of their sons

Harry and Joseph Rappaport

The book is an abridged translation
of the original in German:
Constantin Brunner
Memshelet Sadon
Letztes Wort über den Judenhass und die Juden.
Verlag Neues Vaterland, E. Berger 4 Co.
Berlin W62 (1920)

We are grateful:

To the 'Internationaal Constantin Brunner Instituut' in the Hague for permission to translate 'Memshelet Sadon' into English and to publish the translation:

To Professor Brian Corman, University of Toronto, for his kindness, advice, and help in readying the manuscript for publication and to Mrs. Linda Corman for her bibliographical assistance.

To the family Rappaport for supporting the translation into English from the German original.

TABLE OF CONTENTS

PREFACE

Constantin Brunner was born to a rabbinic family, of great tradition and fame, in Altona, Germany, on August 27th, 1862. As a young man he went to the rabbinic school in Cologne, but there he left religion for philosophy, out of an inner drive that led him, years later to become the creator of *The Doctrine of the Spiritual Élite and the Multitude*; it is based on the theory of the three faculties of human thought: 'Practical Understanding', 'Spirit', 'Superstition'. His gigantic work plan when completed included the founding of our consciousness, i.e., of human psychology and its manifestations in individual life and in society on the theory of physical all-motion. He never could lose sight of the psychological phenomenon of hate in general and the hatred against Jews in particular, in Germany and in the world, since it is one of the persistent and historically one of the most damaging examples of human hate. Even in its mildest form, it degrades the Jew to a second class human being.

Conscious of his great heritage and the impact that the Jews have had on Western Culture through the Bible and the teachings of Christ, he took the stand of a self-conscious man demanding full political rights and social recognition for the Jews, especially in the light of their achievements. He denounced the grave political dangers caused by one group of citizens inviting the others to become 'Jew-baiters'.

In a book written during the 1st World War, *Der Judenhass und die Juden* (*The Hatred of Jews and the Jews*, Berlin 1919), he concerns himself with 'The State', 'The Political Parties', 'The Racial Theory', 'The Question of Anti-Semitism', and 'What Should the Jews Do'? He advised them to REMEMBER, yet laid accent not on the commemoration of their humiliations and of the continued attempts at their annihilation, but on the deep awareness of the great gifts the Jews have given (and still continue to give) to the world: the Bible and its prophets; Christ, the greatest mystical genius of humanity, whose genuine *Jewish* teachings have shaped Western Culture and the ideas of humanity, equality of people, of men and women, from which sprang the ideas of the democratic state and of socialism.

Though friends of Brunner expected him to return to his main philosophical opus, already a year after issuing *The Hatred of Jews and the Jews,* he published *Memshelet Sadon,* the present book that deals with *human judgment* and proves that it is never 'free.' The intensity with which the author, in countless variations, brings evidence that our judgment is not free, but a continuous pursuit of self-interests is as strong an exhortation as the 'Why beholdest thou the mote that is in thy brother's eye, but considerest not the beam in thine own eye?' (Baba bathra 15b), (Matth. 7:3, 4).

The *historical* role of Judaism and anti-semitism is put before our eyes. Advice is given to Jews (since Jew-haters are impervious to it) by explaining the ways men and women commonly 'think' of each other. Unfortunately, there are very few people who have *a genuine interest of thinking,* of rational, creative thought; the majority follow their prejudices based on pride and self-affirmation.

As to the fate of anti-semitism, Brunner is a realist, and he recognizes that as long as there are Jews, there will be anti-semitism, which (in a satanic way) also helps the survival of

Jews. Yet, he continued to publish a series of books on the hatred of Jews, especially in Germany (see list of C.B. – publications).

In this book the thinker with his historical sense for the effect of ideas on mankind, foresees the evolution of an intoxicating hatred in the German masses that will grow to foster mass-murder of innocents. It occurred, indeed sanctified even by the State, 20 years later. Instead of *national* unity, the State propagated *racial* unity and racial arrogance; thus it changed from democracy to tyranny. Seen in the context of the battle of ideas that rakes mankind, these events are the result of materialism, its shaky 'Theory of Evolution' and the superstitious corollary of the racial betterment of the nation.

Brunner fled to Holland and died in the Hague before its occupation by the Nazis; his books were burned in their auto-dafés and his 82 year-old wife Leoni, as well as his daughter Lotte, were deported from Holland and gassed at Sobibor. They, as well as the six million Jews, confirmed by their cruel fate *that the great scourge affecting humanity is HATRED*; it is caused mainly by the *tyranny of pride* among individuals, societies and nations.

Memshelet Sadon starts with a detached psychological analysis of human judgment and ends up shattering all the naive opinions we have in judging our fellow men and women; it is a harrowing safari through the wildernesses of our 'soul.' We are led to understand the old Hebrew precept 'Judge not, that you be not judged' (Sanh. 100). (Matth. 7: 1,2). Brunner's findings are based here not on moral or religious feelings, but on the scientific knowledge that we are continually moved beyond our awareness by waves from the sea of all motion of which our existence is part. Still, hope is entertained that changes in the *interests* of our society may occur which will help decrease the popularity of hating Jews.

To approach then the idea of 'human brotherhood,' one has to distrust any adjudgment of others beings (individuals, societies, nations), since it expresses rather our changing interests than true knowledge. Last but not least, one has to learn to seal one's lips to the surging moralizing word.

THE EDITOR

1.

ON HUMAN JUDGMENT*

If we are to talk seriously about antisemitism, the hatred of Jews, we must examine its basis. That is, we must examine the judgments expressed with regard to Jews. In the first place, therefore, we must understand the way judgments of any kind are reached, and this will occupy the whole of the first chapter. Let the reader not be irritated by this more general discussion, for only in this way can we attain an absolutely firm vantage-point from which to view our particular topic.

What do people ordinarily mean by 'judgment'?

Ordinarily they mean process of thought which, independently of any practical-egoistic interest on the part of the person judging, and determined simply by factors arising from knowledge's relationship to the known object, utters some kind of understanding about this object, whether affirming or denying, approving or disapproving, attributing qualities or excluding them, and by determining its value finally coming to a decision. Hence, too, we speak of the judicial verdict, the impartial judgment of a court, the acquittal or conviction of the accused. According to this ordinary view of

---

* Captions and Running Heads by the editor.

'judgment', since the latter is nothing but the relation of knowledge to some known object, we are only concerned with truth and error. If, by using my mental functions in knowing, I know the truth, my judgment is true. If I err in my knowing, the judgment is erroneous.

But this judgment concerning judgment is itself erroneous, if we consider the judgments men ordinarily arrive at. For we see that they are by no means reached solely through the truth or error of knowledge, otherwise there would not be these stubbornly and persistently opposed judgments and parties, each pursuing their own interests. Interest: that's the word; there we have it! For we see interests determining judgments much more frequently than the converse: judgments governing interests. In all matters of immediate importance to them, most people act according to their own interests. Or else they repeat the customary judgments of their own circle (and this too usually ministers to their own interests since they live in these circles and do well to keep in agreement with them); and those who do not follow ancient custom follow the new custom, to which they attribute exaggerated importance and which justifies their prejudice, their need for freedom or their libertinism. The new wig has as little to do with thought as the old; the head may not visibly sport falsehood, but it harbours it within.

It appears that what determines the judgments of men is the sum total of their interest: the interests of love, of possession, and of prestige, i.e., of honour-vanity. These three, love, possession and prestige, subsume all egoistic interests.

They are the roots of egoism: of these, love unites men, possession and prestige have a divisive effect. Through love (because of the egoism of the lovers) the difference, the being different and having different possession, that is, the interest and the 'I' and the 'thou' (prestige) and the interest of the 'mine' and 'thine' (possession) is, to a certain extent, evened out and cancelled. Thus people are united. Whereas, where love is not present, the interest of possession and prestige, of honour-vanity, separates people and sets them against one another, driving them to pride, contempt, envy and quarrelling, to deception, hatred, persecution and wars.

No one denies that the love interest unites people. Everyone knows and feels that love itself is nothing other than the desire for union. Nor will anyone deny that judgment is influenced by the interests of love, that love exaggerates. No one sees Jack and Jill in the light in which they see each other when they are in love. We also recognize that judgment is influenced by the interests of and the differences due to property, which gives rise to divisions between men; some have what others do not have and would like to have, and this drives them apart and into conflict against each other. But the interests of prestige also determine judgment to no less an extent than love and possession. All other factors making for disunity not arising from the interest of possession, come from the interest of prestige, of honour-vanity. Everyone is constantly presented with this fact together with its consequences, yet the fact is not recognized in its full significance. It is not recognized as the cause of the effects from which all men suffer, the source of their most terrible tortures. Everyone knows it and yet no one is aware of it. Everyone follows suit and makes the others suffer, and no one knows what he is doing, nor does he realize who and what he is on the basis of the motives of his own actions. The prestige interest is everyone's most obscure region, and theoretically difficult to fathom. However, since it is incumbent upon us to show how judgment is affected by interest – for this is the only way to reach firm ground in our present topic, antisemitism, in which the interests of prestige play the chief role – we are bound to tackle the problems of prestige interest, vast as they are. Honour and vanity interpenetrate in the prestige interest as if they were one interest and a single concept (which, however, they seem not to be). In trying to consider honour by itself, as the prime element of the prestige interest, we find that even honour is not a unitary concept and thus hardly capable of being defined.

At first we see honour only from its negative side. When we speak of a man of honour, a man with a good reputation, we generally mean not that this man *has* something that makes him honourable, but that he has *nothing* deserving of disgrace. The good reputation is seldom as good as ill-repute is evil. While a man still has a good name, people do not whisper as many good things about him as they do evil things if he loses his reputation.

And yet our usage is decidedly positive throughout: a man *loses* the good reputation or the honour he formerly *possessed.* What is it then that one has and what does one lose in losing honour? Indeed, in losing honour man loses the most important thing, and practically everything else along with it. For honour is the personality's standing among and with the others, in community. Having honour, one *has* membership in the community and losing honour one *loses* this membership in the community. Without this membership and status among others the personality cannot attain to its full rights, its full life; even if he has love and possessions, such a person is extinguished: he is civically dead. Thus the man who has been 'deprived' of his honour has not been deprived of anything he actually possessed, of anything conferred upon him or given to him in the manner of love and possession. What he has lost, however, is the essentially best part of what he *is*, of his personality, in its standing with the other personalities. Thus he has lost something far more difficult to recover than lost love or lost possessions. Without this status, without this reflection of his personality, mirrored back from the circle of his fellow-personalities, even possessions and love lose much of their intrinsic value, and life itself is no longer worth much. For what is life, merely in itself, to the human being who cannot live in loneliness and for whom life in community, in society, is the very condition of living?

This is the ultimate reason behind the honour interest:

its usefulness for life, which is the more secure and agreeable the more one is honoured; without honour it is not worth living. 'Better honour without life than life without honour.' Life without honour is no life at all, for such a life lacks a personality that it can present to others, and only in this way can the real personality within us receive its outward sphere of action, its free existence, its life. For the Romans, *capitis diminutio* signified the loss of freedom, honour and standing within the law, in others words, civic death. And civic death is in fact a kind of death sentence (*poena capitalis*), by analogy with the *capitis amputatio*; like the death sentence, the punishment of civic death is a punishment which touches life itself, killing the soul while the body lives on. It also resembles natural death in that it puts an end to the external relations of the life of the personality, life in the society of the free. Society thus punishes its members in their very lives because they belong to it, because it, society, is the sum and total interaction of its members. It is only through society that they receive their life. All members of society belong to society, because society is useful to them in this most important matter, in assuring their life. The honour of the members also belongs to society. Honour then is primarily nothing other than that belonging to society which puts all its members under an obligation. Since society consists of honourable personalities, each honourable personality belongs to society. Consequently, mere honourableness in itself secures no special credit.

No one is bound to give praise and recognition to anyone else because of his honourableness. This is why self-praise is intolerable. Furthermore, no one listens seriously to the praise of others, or at most after they have died – for then it makes sense to lament the fact that society has lost a member. But this regret and sorrow does not go very deep, for these members are replaced by others. Since, therefore, society is a society of persons committed to honourable conduct and has to maintain itself as such, it assumes the right to punish the guilty, i.e., anyone who has rendered himself unworthy of belonging among the honourable personalities. Society can totally expel such a person from his natural or civic life, from social status, or it can restrict this status and hence restrict his life's freedom.

If this is so, we must 'guard our honour' if we want to hold on to the freedom of our life. We must not do or permit any infringement of the laws and mores, anything that might bring shame or infamy upon us or cause us disgrace, entailing civic death. If we have done or permitted anything of this kind, it must be concealed and, if it comes to light, we must deny it (*si fecisti, nega*). We must avoid all suspicion of improper conduct and we must not allow ourselves to be insulted or slandered. Most to be feared, after injury to ourselves by dishonourable conduct or neglect, or causing ourselves to appear in a bad light, are insults and slanderings. He who insults us not only speaks or acts against the respect due to our person (thus he *injures*, wounds the personality, gives it pain, and it feels itself slighted): very likely he also prompts others to do the same. And as for the slanderer who attacks us from behind by cavilling at our virtues, detracting from our merits, enlarging and making horrible our faults, making mountains out of molehills and imputing evil to us – his main purpose is to degrade us at all points and render us contemptible. We must fear calumnies and insults; hence we must make ourselves feared, so that people will be slow to trouble us. We must make people afraid of our anger, or – if this is powerless – of our hatred and revenge. We must defend ourselves against insults and slanders with all available means, by our own efforts and, if it comes to it, by claiming the public protection of the law. Brinz (*Pandekten* I. p. 516): 'No one has a right to respect, just as no one has a right protecting him from contempt; on the other hand everyone has a right to be protected from the expression of contempt.'

This quotation once again stresses the completely negative character of honour. But this brings us only to the comma in our sentence, not to its end. We must go further and note that this negative character is only the general, objective side of the phenomenon: for their part, society's subjects all constantly strive to be honoured positively, in two ways. Even mere membership of society, which is experienced above all as membership in a more circumscribed community, is felt to be something positively honourable: the community to which one belongs is something very special. The members of this community – equal in this respect, i.e., not distinct from one another – evince self-esteem in belonging to their community and pride and contempt towards other communities. But even within the particular community each one strives to be positively honoured, to be respected more than other people.

And the reason why so few succeed in this is precisely because all strive for it, each one for himself. No one is seriously interested in giving honour to someone else, even if he deserves it. ('Honour to whom honour is due'? Deathly silence to whom honour is due; dishonour to whom honour is due; and finally honour to whom honour is due when he is no more, when he is no longer alive!) At most, people give honour in order to receive honour back, and when they have some (real or ideal) interest in the other person's honour. Apart from these cases, people are slow to accord positive honour to those they know or who affect their sphere of interest. If they do, it is mostly in a more or less hypocritical way: once the honoured man turns his back, they give vent on the subject of his dishonour and their own honour. There is not a single man who is content to have equal standing with others, to live free of disgrace and keep clear of insults and slanders: everyone wants to go beyond negative free existence and attain positive free existence. Everyone wants to go beyond being in society's debt and reach a situation in which society owes something to him, i.e., the situation of positive honour. So we have arrived at a complete answer to our question as to what is honourable about honour: negatively, it is membership of society and the safeguard of the personality; positively, it is the importance of the person. No one is satisfied merely not to lose his honour, i.e., his membership of society: he wants to gain honour, he wants his membership to be a matter of his personal importance. (This is expressed in the German word for honour, *Ehre*, which comes from the Old High German, 'shining metal,' connected with the words for ore and ice; in Gothic: *ais-tan*; in Latin: *aes-tumare*; in Hebrew: *kabod*; 'radiance,' 'weight,' 'momentousness'). Everyone wants respect for his personality, recognition and praise for his deeds. Just as man's God is (for he has made God in his own image), so man himself is; and man's God wants to be praised for his magnalia, for all his works.

His works praise him, his works are his honour; instead of 'God', the Bible speaks of 'the glory (honour) of God.' Habakkuk 2:14 quotes Isaiah 11:9, and where Isaiah speaks of 'God', Habakkuk speaks of 'the glory of God'. It is praise that makes God to be God. God is what he is praised to be, and man is what he is praised to be. So therefore man is not yet a personality under the conditions of negative honour; he only becomes so under the conditions of positive honour. Life in ill-repute is no life; but even the man who is simply no longer praised takes no pleasure in his life. Fundamentally, everyone wants to be praised simply for existing – and this points to the substratum, the underlying depths, i.e., the immeasurable significance and the eternal value of each existence! However, people do not become aware of this at so noble a level; they strive for a positive, good reputation and to be praised for their virtues and achievements. This striving for honour turns into vanity, which demands immoderate recognition and admiration for its virtues and achievements of value, and even for those that are worthless and those that are pure self-delusion. Finally such people become arrogant, that is, blind with regard to their own worth, with an unrestrained desire for recognition, disdaining and showing contempt for others. All men are like this, I say; all, without exception, even those who think I am not referring to them. Pride is the festering spot in the human animal.

So I am not only speaking of the evidently vain Johnnies and fame-seekers (and there are many of them, and ambition causes more pain than is usually realized) or the strutting show-offs who are happy to be envied for their possessions even if it involves danger. Nor am I only speaking of the countless people who are touchy about external status or position in society on the basis of ancestry, class or rank, office, title, distinction, popularity, or who want to be picked out on account of their achievements, their real or imaginary superiority, talents, merits, their physical strength, beauty, clothes, toilette or fashion. A person may set no store whatsoever on external prestige and yet be extremely vain. Nor should we forget the class of genuinely ambitious people who are simply too inert and sleepy to bother to seek glory – and they are often even more vain that those who have found the glory they were looking for, dealing more haughtily with those round them and more superciliously with those above them. What I am saying also applies to those who have (so to speak) no ambition at all, no vanity and no craving for applause. For all men want their cleverness to be recognized. That is why they are always ready to unpack their opinions, to give their judgment on any issue, to proffer their advice. How often do we hear people saying things like: 'I always knew it! Wasn't that the first thing I said?' This is egoism's common mode of speech; this is the way everyone continually puts himself forward to be recognized and admired as the clever person he is, even if he never gets an honest affirmative answer. He interprets every hypocritical nod of the head on the part of his helpless listener as agreement. He even interprets pure silence in the same way. And it is even more important for everyone's moral character to be acknowledged. The blackest criminal under sentence of death still tries to give the impression that he is better than he is, and the most benighted person, to whom no one listens, does not weary of trying to let his light shine. Everyone persistently displays his personal inner worth, his cleverness and moral character, without shame or qualm, with delicacy and with coarseness, directly or indirectly, often by the most circuitous route, positively or negatively. Everyone is constantly talking or singing in this vein, and it is far from being music to our ears.

We pause here, having reached the danger-point of honour-vanity, *pride*, which (not for nothing) has been regarded as the first of the seven deadly sins. It must be seen, not as a failing on the part of this or that person, but as something inherent in everyone. Consequently it keeps the whole of society in a constant state of extreme danger: nothing is so dangerous to society as pride. Once again, however, it is important for us to recognize pride's universal scope, and to this end we must retrace our steps from honour's positive interest within the community to its apparently merely negative interest associated with membership of the community. If we look more closely we shall see that the interest associated with this membership makes a very strong positive claim, and, as we have already indicated, it does not come out directly and lead to pride versus one's fellows, but leads to pride and arrogance towards those who are different, towards other communities. We shall only grasp the universal scope and power of pride if we devote sufficient attention to the pride involved in this membership interest.

The individual does not have to display an arrogant look or play with the *musculus superbus* of his lower lip; he does not need to offend the sense of honour of those around him by his queer notion and make himself ridiculous and odious; he does not need to attract attention by his malicious talk nor take special part in the gossipy stories and criticisms of his dear fellow human beings; he does not need to assert that 'his excrement is sweet spice'. He may even appear to be the most modest and most humble person and even to be a *calumniator sui*, one of those who are eternally dissatisfied with themselves, a self-depreciator, self-torturer and self-slanderer, as it were. He can still satisfy his pride within the clique or group to which he attributes himself, in the broadest generality of his religion, his nation, his race, by moralizing in general terms about 'the others'. Our religion is the only true one, the absolutely moral religion which satisfies the demands of the intellect. Our nation, our race is more gifted and more moral than the other nations and races! We are prime specimens of humanity, and as for the others, they are – simply lower grade! Everyone has this urge to be superior to others, either by elevating oneself or by pulling them down; not everyone does the first, but everyone does the second.

Not everyone can really elevate himself visibly by his life, his deeds and opinions, and it is bad enough that people do not like hearing others praise their own worth – for everyone only likes to hear himself praised. On the other hand people like to hear others being belittled, for this lowering of others makes the audience feel elevated just like the speaker. They benefit by what is taken from the others; the night gains what the day loses.   There is no one, however evil and contemptible he is himself, who does not despise someone else. How much scorn there is in the world as a result of the pride of the scorners!   No man living is safe from contempt; he only needs to be alive to be despised (and he only needs to die to be praised and given the 'last honours' by those who, in his lifetime, would never give him so much as a 'first honour'). Just as all men experience being despised, so they are all scorners themselves.

As we have said, pride does not need to find expression through downright insolence.   For the most part, community and communal pride, group pride, is much more effective in generating contempt.   It profoundly rends society apart in long standing enmities.   We only have to think how genuinely all human beings despise each other–and all are right to do so: since they all arrogantly despise each other, they are all despicable.   In their reciprocal scorn they despise themselves, their own human nature, and that renders them contemptible. It is true: all human beings despise each other under some heading or other, whether they be races, nations, parties, classes, professions.   The generations despise each other: youth scorns age and vice versa.   In our day, with its pride unleashed on a hitherto unknown scale, it is the young and immature who express their hostility to their elders in the most unrestrained manner, both theoretically and in practice. (In this connection we are bound to think of today's little men in the world of art who, with their immaturity and crudity, think themselves superior to the great artists.) Contempt remains, whereas appreciation is usually transitory. Appreciation is a reciprocal matter and men are so easily 'insulted', which immediately vitiates it (this also occurs through the interest arising from some new appreciation). Contempt, however, is generated without any reciprocity, without the person scorned doing anything, without his lifting a finger, without his learning of the contempt heaped on him. And even in the few cases where there is a significant appreciation of value, not based on mutual interest, an appreciation that is lasting because it is founded on higher reasons – i.e., when no one has any interest in despising the persons concerned because they are dead, or because they have managed to 'make it' in their lifetime and so have become figures to be respected – clearly, I am talking about mankind's geniuses – even in cases such as these, where there is a belated appreciation of such persons, it is usual for it to be preceded by the worst kind of contempt, ridicule, calumny and hate-inspired persecution. People reserve their fiercest contempt for those of their fellow men who most provoke them to thought. What about those men of great character and stature? It is of no avail. Value has nothing to do with being despised or not being despised. Socrates, Christ and Spinoza were the most infamous men of their times; Spinoza was accursed, Christ was crucified, Socrates was poisoned – because of their alleged spiritual inferiority and moral unworthiness. Even the most stupid person should see from this that it is not only those who are really spiritually inferior and morally unworthy and corrupt who are despised; even the best can be despised and hated, precisely because they are the best (*veritas odium parit*), because they want to show that the others are not good enough and do not think aright. But they were not prepared to be shown any such thing; *they* showed *them*! They were not improved by the influence of the best; in fact, these best people irritated them and brought the worst out of them, just as silver chloride turns black when exposed to light. The fact that they poisoned, crucified and cursed Socrates, Christ and Spinoza shows the evil that was in them.

Contempt on the basis of pride plays the most significant part; thought plays the smallest role; indeed, in contempt it has no role at all. Man only thinks when motivated by some interest, and then what thinks in him is only the ideation of his interest. He has nothing but his interest, he has no real thought, only his interest's ideatum. But since the root remains hidden and he is conscious of the ideatum of his interest as thinking, he takes the ideatum of his interest to be the free interest of thought, he takes it to be thinking. His main interest, however, next to those of love and possession, is his honour-vanity, his ego in comparison and relation with others. His main concern is to be recognized for his value and his sense of his own value, to be accepted for what he is or believes himself to be, or what others ought to believe him to be. He wants to appear to be what he is not, to appear clever and of a 'moral' character. This interest on the part of honour-vanity generates a noli-me-tangere attitude in everybody;

however many others he knows to be spiritually inferior and morally unworthy, let anyone dare to approach him and impugn his honour by suggesting the same about him! Honour-vanity is the real, personal, gigantic, central issue; as we have already said, it is mirrored, in colossal proportions, in the image of man's God: here man can best read off his own nature. This God must be honoured and praised, and there is nothing else of which he is so jealous, nothing else which makes him so vengeful, even going as far as damning for all eternity those who blaspheme him. This is the prestige interest: as we have seen, it is the most important interest of man in community. Honour, repute, is by no means a highly-valued nothing: it is really and truly everything in our here-and-now life among our fellow men; it is our interest in making our personality secure. Consequently, it is our interest in elevating our personality; and this is very useful for society since it gives rise to many things which would not be there without the stimulus of this interest, this vanity: *la vertu n'irait pas si loin, si la vanité ne lui tenait compagnie.* However. First of all, society is of use to the individual, then the individual is of use to society, and the next thing is that he harms society. Prestige interest also contains within it the greatest danger for the life of the community, for it leads men, all men, to go beyond the negative, i.e., security, via the positive, i.e., superiority, to a positively unrestrained attitude characterized by pride and arrogance toward other human beings. This applies to all people, all people! Let no one imagine that he is without pride, that he has no part in contributing to the danger inherent in human pride. There is a core of pride in every man, pouring its baneful gleam and stench over other human beings and over the whole humanity. Prestige interest and the pride that goes with it—this indeed constitutes an interest determining judgment no less than the interests of love and possession. If we could set these three: *prestige, love and possession* (the sub-individuals within the individual man) against each other, it would be hard to say whether one would win out against the others. And as for the hotheads who have set themselves to dream up a society in which the possession interest would no longer lead to dissension and crime, they have embraced a doubly mistaken ideal; for no society of the kind could ever be established, and even if it were, and the dangers of possession were eliminated, pride would really come into its own and nothing would be any the better. One thing is certain: pride determines judgment, which thereby loses its value as judgment, for instead of containing simply the relationship of knowing to the known, it also includes a relationship to interest, the chief interest of the person judging in his relationship to the issue he is judging.

The usual judgments are judgments of interest and they tell us less about the nature of the person judged than about the interest of the one who judges. This is a truth to be preserved in our arsenal, and we should entirely discard the view that the common judgments of men and the judgments of common men (and hence of practically all men) are just functions of knowing, isolated from physical human existence, and concerned simply with truth and error.

This view comes from the distorted psychology which attributes to knowing, because it *comes to our awareness* in isolation from our other thought-processes, an independent and (what is more) totally mistaken significance, as if it were some faculty of objective cognition. According to true psychology as it is developed in *The Doctrine of the Spiritual Élite and the Multitude*, judgment belongs to the totality of human consciousness; it is part of the unity of feeling, knowing and willing, and this unity and totality has no other significance than the practical one of the provident care of our life.

Like all animals, we human beings are so constituted that we have to take measures to preserve our thingly nature and its life. Animal and human consciousness serve this end. Relative consciousness, including judgment and all the thought-processes of our intellect (knowing) is important solely for the business of the provident care of life. In other words, relative consciousness, feeling, knowing and willing, makes it possible for us to maintain our life, i.e., the motion of our thingly existence, within the world's motion. Our consciousness is nothing other than the consciousness of motion, the inner aspect of the motion of our existence, or motion in so far as we become aware of it. For consciousness itself only exists by virtue of the motion of our physical existence. We, with our feelings, are inwardly what we are moved or caused to be, in pleasure or pain. Our doing and willing is that which we want to move or bring about in order to generate and maintain pleasure and keep its opposite at bay or lessen it; or else – as mere willing – it is such motion   or causation in a state of tension.   With our knowing, however, things are supposed to be quite the reverse: our heads are supposed to be able to attain to the pure relation of knowing to the known objects, unrelated to the interest of our feeling and willing, our moving and being moved, i.e., outside the motion of our moving world, in a state of rest, unmotivated by motion: thus we are alleged to be able to objectify our knowing and judging!

The man who can do this is a thinker. He is a man who recognizes that human thinking governed by interest, including his own thinking of that kind, is egoistic non-thinking. In his consciousness, moreover, as well as this interest-motivated thinking, he also has the genuine interest in thinking, he has real thoughts.   In other words, he is a man who has not immersed himself, like other men, in relativity, in the world of thingly motion; his thinking does not pour only into externals, into the ideatum of things, but into his inner self, into his own depths, reflecting on the absolute nature of his authentic being. Men in general, however, are not thinkers, and cannot make their knowing any more objective than their feeling and willing. Men are men; they are not mirrors. They are human through and through, and even at the apex, in knowing, they are not mirrors. What they know is not some miraculous mirror-image of the object which – even more miraculously – can sometimes turn out to be a distorted mirror-image: the sum total of their knowledge is nothing but an inventory of what serves or harms their interest. Their knowing is only knowing on account of their interested willing in the service of their interested feeling.

(They have knowledge of things, of motion, so that they can will and act, i.e., move in such a way that they can feel, i.e., be moved in a way that gives them pleasure.) Thus their knowing itself is governed by interest. Interest never disappears from the relative consciousness, which is nothing but our relative existence itself and its business of self-preservation; our relative, thingly existence is linked to our interest in this existence, and our entire relative consciousness is nothing but this interest. Even the knowledge aspect of our thinking as found in our consciousness has no further significance than this; there can be no question of an objective cognitive element in the knowledge aspect of the human mind. It is impossible for men who have entirely immersed themselves, with their relative consciousness, in the world's motion and thus discern nothing from within but their part of the world's motion (and we only see the rest of it from outside), who, with all their interests, do not get beyond themselves, their own pleasure and pain – it is impossible for a man of this sort, with his relative consciousness, to seek anything but his own advantage when he makes a judgment.

'This is why it is so hard to clarify and refute one judgment by another: for ultimately it is no judgment at all but the irrefutable interest of our egoism. Ultimately it is not judgment but advantage.'[1] This explains why men so rarely manage to convert others to their judgments and opinions, which usually means moving someone else to

---

[1] Der Judenhass und die Juden, 2nd and 3rd editions, p. 288.

embrace our advantage and his own disadvantage. We can understand why truth, on the whole, has no effect on human beings. For truth's entire treasure-house is at our disposal, and rays of light must stream forth upon mankind from truth's perfection: but rivers of darkness well up from interest and pride, covering men's eyes. Consequently, there is no other answer to the ancient question as to whether virtue (= truth) can be taught or is innate, than this: *what is innate is interest*; while virtue can certainly be taught, it cannot be learned if it is opposed by interest! Truth finds it so difficult to stand against accepted judgment because, while judgment is part of knowing, it is by no means solely concerned with truth and error. For it is far more than mere knowing: it is the totality of those interests within our knowing which preserve life or allegedly preserve it; the interests are only within our knowing so that this knowing can be used as a tool by them. The dominant factors are interest, drives and passions; reason, the intellect, is the maid-of-all-work (who naturally, when she is not needed, goes for an occasional walk by herself). As for reason restraining the drives, usually there is as much hope of this as of the horse reining in the coachman. For the drives do the steering, reason is the one driven. We must entirely give up the dictum formulated by our pride, namely, that man is the rational being. If we look at man and his history we could just as well call him the irrational being, the being given to the folly of self-deception (for in his self-deception, and due to his fancied moralism, he forfeits practically all understanding of his actual egoistic self).

Man is distinguished from the other animals only through his incomparably more extensive interest and his incomparably greater rationality and irrationality. Every animal has reason in its own degree – reason is what enables the animal to survive – but no animal harms its own species by so much unreason as man, and mostly as a result of his pride and hatred arising from moralistic criticism. (If we want to use the word 'moral' in the usual sense, we must say that man is morally the lowest of all animals; for he is the torturer and murderer of every possible animal, of myriad other species. To some extent he does this out of the interest of sheer necessity, but largely out of the unrestrained interest of his own pleasure. He is also the one who tortures and murders within his own species, out of the conviction that he is better than his brothers and sisters. We are the most immoral animals because we cultivate moralism, and the most irrational because the interest of the moment overwhelms us.) In the presence of interest, man forgets all reason; he literally forgets his former interests once he no longer has them. Thus he becomes intolerant or at least impatient with his dearest, even with his children, e.g., with their noise and fidgeting, in spite of the fact that he was once a child. But how little do we learn from our own childhood about how to manage children! We who never learn except by experience, do not even learn these things from experience; we not only act, we also judge, according to our own interests. Judgment has so little objective relationship to its object that it varies according to the interests of the moment. Two persons judging the same object will, according to their individual interests, arrive at opposite conclusions, both convinced of the correctness of their judgments and each proving with utmost clarity that his opponent is mistaken.   Convictions and judgments are formed by one's interests, and the diverse judgments given with regard to some identical matter, grounding hatred on one side and love on the other, clearly proclaim the fact that they are judgments of interest, i.e., not judgments at all, but interests. Hatred could never arise from a judgment in a thinking man, only from some interest in a non-thinking man, through the frustration of his interest as a result of some injury (real or imaginary) to it. Hatred has as little to do with judgments as physical pain, and, like the latter, it is always nothing but a reaction to some life-inhibiting factor (as is anger, repugnance and loathing). With regard to these so-called judgments and thoughts, we must believe not only that interest plays a part, but that interest is totally involved, affecting the very last trace of consciousness. We must reckon with the emptiness of every true judgment in the thought-process; we must believe in the complete absence and impossibility of the first and last qualities demanded of a person who judges, namely, a real will to truth. Or, if we cannot believe in conscious self-deception, on the part of such a non-thinker, for the sake of his interest, we can at least accept his readiness to believe implicitly and employ the deceit practised by others in so far as it serves his own interest.

This is particularly the case where hatred is concerned. For everyone is interested only in his own interest, and the more his passions are involved, the more eagerly and blindly he will grasp to left and to right for material with which to feed them. The one who hates, who hates blindly, mortally, who has been injured by the person he hates or believes that he is injured, threatened or obstructed by him, wants to wound him in return. He wants to render him harmless, and is not particular about the means to be used. This is true of the individual who hates, and almost more true of hating communities (one nation against another, one group in society against another). Communities of this kind are totally blind in their self-interest. With their misbegotten judgments they have no ability to distinguish right from wrong except in so far as their interest is right and that of the others is wrong; they use moralistic clichés to rationalize the worst injustice. Men are forever doing two things at the same time: acting egoistically and talking moralistically. Egoism never lacks the musical accompaniment of moralism. Everyone is like this; everyone is an egoist and a moralist. Do you think you have to deal with a single person? Never think that; you always have to deal with two people, an egoist and a moralist. By 'moralist' I mean the egoist in the theatrical role of moralism. Where are the honest people who do not try to justify their egoistic actions by adducing moral reasons? (And in many cases they even believe this themselves, all the more since no one needs to learn the role of moralist or have recourse to moralism's box of cosmetics – for by nature moralism belongs with egoism.) Nor do we lack examples of evil deeds where the evil-doers accuse their victims of being evil, and think of themselves as the good ones. Moralistic criticism, i.e., asserting that I am good and that someone else is bad, is part and parcel of egoism. We can assume that only in rare cases are those hated, be they individuals or communities, really as black as they are painted in the judgment of those – the white ones – who hate them.

2.

THE ANTI-SEMITIC JUDGMENT

What then of the antisemitic judgment on Jews? Essentially, it is that Jews are spiritually inferior and morally degenerate human beings. These are the two accusations – are they not? – to which man's prestige interest, his honour-vanity, is most sensitive; he rejects them because they imply the most serious threat to his personality and freedom. Does this judgment, that Jews are spiritually inferior and morally degenerate, express the truth about them, or – and our former observations should have prepared us for this possibility – is this judgment on the part of the anti-Semites merely a judgment arising from interest?

Possibly, the Jews might not be the substantial cause of the antisemitic judgment against them, the hatred and persecution of them. They could be simply the incidental cause, the trigger which sets it off, the stimulus unleashing that hostility against his fellows which is latent in man, always ready to break out, and which thus is let loose against the Jews.

In this case the hatred of Jews, a form of hatred of mankind, would seem to spring from the same root as we find in the nature of all human beings; of all ordinary human beings, that is, whose life consists in nothing other than the interest of their love, possessions and prestige, their honour-vanity, ending in pride. (The exception are the real thinkers, who do not think solely their thingly-human interest; and by 'thinkers' I mean all spiritual people, whether productive or reproductive, receptive, all who are good or have become so.) This root of hostility towards one's fellows is found in Jews just as much as in other people, and we can assume that, under similar historical conditions, if Jews formed the majority in our countries and there were a minority of non-Jews living among them, the latter would meet the same fate as Jews are now encountering. In such a case antisemitism would be a particular instance of hatred of mankind triggered off by Jews who, inwardly essentially similar to other men, merely provide the occasion and object of this hatred because of their external difference from their environment, particularly because of their distinctive appearance and names. Everywhere they are found, they are 'the others', not least on account of their specifically Jewish names, and this very otherness would suffice to bring the antisemitic interest-judgment down upon them, a judgment which would say more about anti-Semites than about Jews.

This might be the situation, but we cannot yet be sure.

It is also possible that the anti-Semites' judgment on Jews does
not arise from interest or pride, but is truth: perhaps in the
Jewish race we really do have a spiritually inferior and morally
degenerate race of people that exercises a baneful influence on
mankind. Experience must decide: the proof of the pudding is
in the eating, not in studying. And the anti-Semites, who are
not strong on study, concentrate on saying that they have tested
this issue and proved that they are right. What can we do,
confronted with the proof adduced by antisemitism?

Prove the contrary.

But we do not need to undertake this proof; we do not
need even to begin to prove it. In any case it would not be so
easy to prove our case as for the anti-Semites to prove theirs.
How could we set it up?   We cannot have a scientific
experiment on the Jewish issue by 'changing the conditions'.
We cannot synthesize little Jews and operate on them as on
poor frogs.   Nor can we capture fully-grown Jews in their
natural state, put them together with non-Jews in their natural
state and then observe the effects of the Jewish minds upon
non-Jews. Fortunately, however, there is an experiment that
operates automatically and proves the contrary. In fact there
are two contrary proofs, a major one and a minor one. These
totally discredit the anti-Semites' proof and show that the Jews
cannot by any means be rightly called less gifted or worse than
other human beings; indeed they show that the Jews very much
belong to the human race. These two contrary proofs enable
us to discover the truth about the Jews and to establish with

precision the effects of which they are actually the cause. These two proofs are evident to all who have eyes to see. (For there are also eyes that do not see because they do not want to see. Galileo had constructed a telescope and through it observed Jupiter's moons, but the scholars of his time had an interest in not believing in Jupiter's moons: they refused to look through the telescope and so saw nothing.)

The minor proof is continually being made. We do not need to look through a telescope; we only need to look around us: everywhere we see how gifted Jews, gifted in every possible way, acquire recognition and renown just as much as non-Jews. More Jewish scholars have received the Nobel Prize for scientific endeavour than those of France and England together (and incidentally no antisemitic scholar has received the Nobel Prize). Quite clearly, the world's actual interest in the benefits coming from Jewish talent is greater than the judgment of antisemitism, greater than all the other anti-Jewish prejudice which, though not explicitly antisemitic, is widely found. In the face of this irrefutable wealth of talent, therefore, the notion that Jews are spiritually inferior is clearly nonsense and we need say no more about it; the antisemitic assertion collapses when confronted with the world's consistent experience of Jews. This alone would show that what we have here is a judgment with no truth behind it, arising from antisemitic interest, quite apart from the far more significant facts we shall come to in the big proof.

For the moment, however, let us stay with the minor proof disproving the second point of the antisemitic judgment, namely, that Jews are morally degenerate. This affirmation too is refuted everywhere by the actual conditions of life, unmasking the antisemitic judgment and showing it to be an interest-inspired judgment, i.e., not a judgment dependent on truth or error, but an interest. It is the interest or supposed interest of the anti-Semite, the interest or supposed interest of the anti-Semite's possession or honour-vanity. Where the interest of possession or honour-vanity is not so evident as in the case of anti-Semites, it does not mean that the Jews are inferior, that they are morally degenerate or less talented; it does not follow that they have to be persecuted or kept at a distance. The interest of possession can work in the opposite direction, in such a way that people are anxious to have connections with Jews; i.e., if collaboration and friendly relations with Jews promises some gains. There are many instances of this, where the relationship between Jews and indebted non-Jews is the same – neither better nor worse – than that between other men and those indebted to them; as if there were no antisemitic judgment at all. Antisemitism does not always and everywhere raise its head, as it must if antisemitism represented a valid and true judgment about Jews.

Indeed, there is an interest arising from possession that is able to convert people from antisemitism and make them rue and forget all their antisemitism: now antisemitism seems falsehood; everything looks different once the golden lamp is lit.

But we cannot by any means assume that anti-Semites act hypocritically out of the lust for profit, right up to the extreme of marrying a Jewess. Thus for instance, if a nobleman who previously has been antisemitic seeks to marry a rich Jewess and actually marries her, we must assume that the interest of possession, i.e., an interest proving stronger than the antisemitic judgment, has drawn him away from his antisemitic passion for virtue. It is a question of the stronger interest, in other words it depends on the interest, not the judgment. It is never a question of judgment, not even in the case of children, who are now being mobilized and pledged to hatred of Jews, as Hamilcar pledged his little Hannibal to hate the Romans – in spite of the fact that children *cannot* have any opinion as to such things as 'the Jewish question', as is agreed by their adults, who also have no opinion on the matter. But, good Christians that they are, they let the children come to them for sweet-smelling instruction; all the same a little filth can be mixed in and given to the pure, childlike souls; pride, hatred and arrogant behavior towards Jews can be inculcated into them. In the end, however, as we read in the splendid story by old Johann Peter Hebel, children have no other interest than their own, childish interest, and under certain circumstances they can renounce the mischievous training they have been given. 'Every week,' Hebel tells us, 'a Hebrew of the Sundgau passed on business through a certain village. Every week the mischievous urchins would call after him through the whole village: "Jew! Jew! Jew-kike!" The Hebrew thought, what shall I do?

If I shout back at them, they will shout all the worse, and if I throw something at them, I shall get twenty back. But one day he brought a lot of newly-minted white Basle centimes with him, five of which are equivalent to two farthings, and gave one to each boy who shouted "Jew-mouth!" at him. When he returned, all the children were standing waiting for him: "Jew! Jew! Jew-kike! Sholem lechem!" Each of them got a centime, and so it happened several times, and the children looked forward to his coming from one week to the next, and even began to grow fond of the kindhearted Jew. But the day came when he said, "Children, I cannot give you any more, however much I would like to, for I find it comes round too soon and there are too many of you." At this, they became very sad, so that the eyes of some of them began to fill with tears, and they said, "If you don't give us any more centimes, we won't call you 'Jew-kike' either." The Hebrew said, "Well, I'll just have to accept it. I cannot make you." So from that hour he gave them no more centimes, and from that hour they let him go peacefully through the village.'

This too was an instance of conversion from antisemitism through possession-interest; and what do you think would happen if all anti-Semites were to get gold from the Jews for their antisemitism (and the leaders, naturally, would get a fixed salary), and if this went on for a long time, and then the Jews stopped giving money? It would be by no means the worst way to undermine antisemitism, at least for a while.

Let us return, however to the anti-Semite who was converted by his financial interest and married the rich Jewess.

How he has changed in the meantime! His conversion has gone much deeper, for now he even loves the Jewess! If put to it, an anti-Semite who has remained an anti-Semite will be able to understand how it is possible to love a Jewish girl whose mouth emits pieces of gold whenever she speaks. But what of a Jewish girl without the pieces of gold? In her case, surely, whenever she opens her mouth, a toad must jump out! And, whether put to it or not, how will an anti-Semite who has not married a gold-plated Jewess understand that such conversion can go further than the realization that loving a Jewess provides better nourishment than antisemitism? That Jewesses, and even Jews, can be loved even without there being any property gain? These are terrible happenings – but they do happen, despite all antisemitic judgments. How are such things possible even once? – and yet they are by no means rare occurrences. These are the really dangerous Jews, the ones who (horrible to relate) can be loved for themselves right from the outset. They are a danger to antisemitism, for this is philosemitism, literally: love of Jews instead of hatred of Jews. But it actually takes place. When Jack loves a Sarah, and she means more to him than the Three Graces and the Nine Muses, does he wonder whether the one who means everything to him ought not to be a Jill? And when Sarah loves Jack in return, it does not occur to her that, according to the Old Testament, Sarah should have her Abraham; perhaps Abraham will find his happiness with a Jill. So even the elemental unifying interest of love can operate between Jews and non-Jews. This applies not only to the interest of sexual love, furthermore, but also to the genuine love of friendship. And not only that – for now the whole thing is out of control, and all hope is extinguished for antisemitism – but it even applies to the profound regard in which people are held in the context of the noblest idealism: there are men and women, non-Jews, people distinguished by virtues and social standing, who are attached by ardent love to a Jew whom they hold to be an uncommon man; they regard it as one of the highest honours bestowed on them that they may come close to him.

Arising out of the interest of possession, of love and of honour, i.e., out of all the interests of life, therefore, there are relationships between non-Jews and Jews in which the Jews are not held by non-Jews to be morally more degenerate and evil than other human beings, relationships just like the ordinary relationships between ordinary people. Moreover, non-Jews are prepared to enter into a relationship of love full of respect and veneration for those unusual Jews in whom the nature of the human being is manifested more fully and finely. Nor are these good relationships rare exceptions, like a contented symbiosis between cat and dog, as it were. In Berlin, from 1899 to 1903, there were 3047 purely Jewish marriages and 1065 mixed marriages with Jews and Jewesses, i.e., 34.95%. So, bearing in mind the small number of Jews and the prejudice that exists against them, the conclusion must be accepted that Jews are human beings like other men. The fact is the Jews exercise a homogeneous influence on non-Jews everywhere, everywhere, that is, where Jews and non-Jews are mutually involved with one another; for the cases of disunity are hardly more frequent than between non-Jews and non-Jews, and *the racial difference does not play even the smallest role in all these relationships, for they are relationships between individuals of one and the same white race.* What has become of the judgment of the anti-Semites? The anti-Semites would have to refute these facts if their judgment were to stand. But to refute facts would mean making facts to be no facts at all. And no one can do that.

So much for our smaller counter-proof and the here-and-now answer to our question, whether Jews really are and do what the antisemitic judgment says they are and do. But behind all this we hear a far more powerful answer; the voice of mankind's history commands us totally to reject the antisemitic judgment. In the face of history and its great counter-argument the antisemitic assessment of the Jews is no more correct than the inane and slandering pronouncements on geniuses. It is no more correct than the verdicts uttered with regard to the crucifixion, the poisoning, and the anathemas suffered by Christ, Socrates and Spinoza. The judgment of their own times on these greatest geniuses of mankind was worthless, and in vain did the educated spokesmen of their times seek to damn the memory of them; history's counter-proof reveals their unexhaustible value. The world discovered that they were by no means spiritually inferior, morally degenerate and a threat to the interest of humanity, as their times had believed, but rather were of the greatest possible service to this interest. The judgment turned into its opposite: the most infamous became the most famous, and the most despised men of their times became the most loved and revered men of all times. And as for the Jews – no doubt some anti-Semite will say that I am raising all Jews, wholesale, to the level of geniuses – all I want to do, in truth, is to show that it is possible to be despised even without being a genius, and that an entire community can be despised in spite of the fact that people receive no less good things from it than from any other community; indeed, in spite of the fact that it has produced the most genial of humanity's gifts!

However despised, in general, the Jews have always been, the world has profited from their achievements. Indeed it must be said that the greatness and renown of these achievements is astonishingly disproportionate to their small numbers (Jews constitute approximately 1/100 of the human race) and their ill repute. Anyone who fails to be astonished at this disproportion between the Jews' honourable and acknowledged influence and the personal dishonour in which they are held, has not yet begun to reflect upon the Jewish phenomenon in the world. Only a very few wonder at this, because only the very few know what is really Jewish in the world; for Jewry's chief achievement is called by a non-Jewish name. In fact, we find the strangest imaginable interplay between Jewish honour and Jewish ignominy in the world, contradicting purely logical judgment and justice, which can only be explained by the presence of two different interests in the world, a superficial interest governed by the senses and an interest at a deeper level which is not concerned about the former and works against it. (To the uneducated – among whom we must reckon not least the ordinary scholars – this must remain completely unintelligible; but anyone who knows human nature will not be surprised to find in humanity what can be found in so many individual human characters: *in those aspects of their life and destiny which have most significance* there is also the warring combination of unfreedom and freedom, and a necessity, which exerts its influence through the course of past history and future, opposing the blindness of its intention and insight.) The deep-level interest whereby the world continues, in fact, to acknowledge the gifts and the moral worth and importance of Jews, gives the lie to its interest-dominated judgment of contempt against the Jews and renders it utterly preposterous.

The endowment and ethos of the Jews (Nietzsche calls the Jewish people the ethical genius among nations) are more important for our cultural life than we can say, as even our Social Democratic movement shows – doubtless one of the greatest movements of history – in which Jews have played a crucial role. And what is without doubt the greatest and most genial factor of mankind's entire history, Christianity, was wholly and exclusively realized by Jews. In saying this we must bear in mind what the word Christianity means: not merely (so to speak) Jewish religion distinguished from the other Jewish religion by its central belief in Jesus as the Messiah who has come, but the foundation of the civilization of our peoples; our culture is Christian, however unchristian or anti-christian, in religious terms, our ideas may be, and all of us are Christians.

Jews did not impose this Christianity on the nations by subterfuge. The reward the wholly Jewish apostles of the Jewish gospel received was quite different from money and thanks[1]; and once the nations had accepted this Jewish gospel, which was the real core of all Judaism – evidently because they had to, feeling that they could not possibly produce anything equivalent on their own – they cheated the Jews of the merit of having produced it. It was that most authentic need, the interest attaching to deep matters, that led to the acceptance of Judaism as the religion that was morally most worthy of mankind; but it was an interest of another kind, on the surface of life, that led to hostility against Jews, conceived as morally degenerate. Thus they were cheated of the credit due to them. The hostile attitude towards Jews and the world's total lack of thought has produced the amazing result that when Christians today speak of Christianity, they practically all think they are speaking of something different from and contrary to Judaism. They imagine they are speaking of something noble as against something ignoble.

---

[1] 'Very few of the apostles escaped taking up and carrying Christ's cross in literal, terrible truth. All of them became cross-bearers of eternal and exemplary importance, glorious heroes of humble discipleship of the Crucified, including those who were not adorned with the purple of the bloody martyr's death. Paul may indeed have received the "forty stripes save one" five times, been beaten with rods thrice and stoned once, and shipwrecked more than three times (2 Cor 11:24,25), giving him the right above all others to say that he bears in his body "the dying of the Lord Jesus" or the marks of his wounds (2 Cor 4:10; Gal 6:17); but in terms of their inner readiness and disposition of hearts all of them were stigmatized in spirit and truth. No saint of subsequent Christian ages can come anywhere near them in this respect, not even those saints who bear the stigmata in their flesh, of whom the Roman Church is so proud.' O. Zöckler, das Kreuz Christi. Gütersloh 1875, S. 116.

In fact, however, Christianity at its noblest is Judaism; the practice of non-Jewish Christianity (in its opposition to Judaism and Jews) was and still is one of unscrupulous looting – not intentionally, of course, but in its effects. Those who recklessly plunder it take all the credit for themselves, abusing and calumniating those they have despoiled and doing all they can to drive them to ruin.

If any reader finds these remarks unjust and exaggerated I can only urge him to read the last section of my book *Der Judenhass und die Juden*; having read this, he will be clearer about the Jews' significance for history. The great imitates the small, and this has never been so true as in the case of the world and Judaism. No men have contributed more to civilization, in the highest sense, than Jews, whom the antisemitic judgment holds to be the worst people, people of inferior endowment. The most influential genius of the world, revered by all our nations as the noblest human phenomenon, is Jesus Christ, the most Jewish of all Jews. Not even the most rabid anti-Semite is venerated anywhere near as highly; in fact, the anti-Semites themselves venerate him and believe in him as the only Jew with whom they could have come to an understanding (because he upbraided the Jews); he would be of one heart and mind with them (because they too rail against Jews) if his spirit were to come down again and indwell a body; they see him running to his heavenly window every minute, delighting in the sweet fragrance of the anti-Semites.

No. We will not go on wondering whether it might somehow be possible. It is impossible that the Jews should really be the cause of the anti-Semites' judgment against them. If it were true that the Jews were spiritually inferior, morally degenerate and had a pernicious influence, it would also have to be true (which it is not) that they exercise this influence on non-Jews, with the result that no non-Jew would associate with them, let alone live alongside them. The world would have long since ceased having any contact with them, and they would have played a correspondingly inferior and evil part in history; the words of their Bible would not be capable of revealing their eternally inexhaustible significance, now as in all former times; this Bible would long since have been thrown on the rubbish-heap. In that case our counter-proofs, the big proof and the smaller proof, refuting all that the antisemitic judgment asserts, could not be true. But they are true, indubitably. There can therefore be no doubt that the arguments of the anti-Semites are invalid. And this in turn convinces us that their experiences were influenced by their judgment, a judgment governed by interest, not answering to the demands of logical and forensic judgment. For the antisemitic judgment of the Jews contains both things: the logical, apodictic judgment, absolutely sure of itself, acknowledged by the person judging as a properly grasped, logical judgment, beyond all doubt, along with the juridical verdict; and this is accompanied by the feeling of frustration and indignation at the fact that this verdict is not universally applied or applicable, that anti-Semites are not given the power of carrying it out.   For the anti-Semites want to be plaintiff, judge and executioner.

In logical and forensic judgments the only relevant factors are truth and error, and every error is ready to be corrected by truth so that it may express the relationship of genuine knowledge to what is to be known. The antisemitic judgment says nothing at all about the Jews it professes to judge, only about the anti-Semites themselves, i.e., about the nature of their interests or supposed interest.   Its point of departure is not truth; it actually offers deep resistance to all truth from start to finish; it is supremely obstinate in its blindness. The human mind and heart knows no worse enemy of truth and love and of all genuine self-perfection than the interest that springs from pride, and this is the chief origin of antisemitism. The allegory of pride shows it blindfolded and with donkey's ears; it is not in the least concerned to improve itself and, if possible, those who are less perfect.   Its sole interest is in appearing perfect or more perfect, cleverer and better than others, belittling others and keeping them humiliated and at arm's length.

Antisemitism comes chiefly from the interest of pride; of that we have no doubt. It does not come from love's interest in union, and so there remains only the divisive interests of honour-vanity and of possession, the supposed interests of unseemly egoism: there remains only the antisemitism that comes from pride and from the jealousy of the possession of a higher standard of living.

The main one is the antisemitism that comes from pride, although, naturally, jealousy should not be underestimated and plays its part in the former. 'What? shall those who are so much worse than we are have possessions among us? Everything they possess belongs to us, the good and the clever. Indeed, we are the good and the clever, our race is good and clever. The Jews are the evil and crafty ones; that is why they have deceived us, who are far too good-natured and unsuspecting. Yes, that's it: our race, all the rest of humanity, is not only good: we are far too good; our patience is unbelievable! We who realize how good and clever we are must take away all that the Jews possess, for the good of mankind!'[2] The main thing, however, is pride, which here stiffens jealousy quite differently and unlike the other case: *one* anti-Semite by reason of the jealousy associated with the Jews making a carefree living creates a hundred anti-Semites by reason of pride. Without pride, there would be no antisemitism, for antisemitism is really and truly a species of the genus pride. This is what antisemitism says: 'We are the

---

[2] Plunder was the main issue in all the pogroms of Jews (since the Crusades). In Hertzog's 'Elsasser Chronik' for the year 1339 we read: 'On this Friday the Jews were caught, and immediately the next morning, Saturday, they were burnt in their churchyard, on a wooden scaffold. There were an estimated two thousand of them. Those who were prepared to be baptized were allowed to live. (But even their possessions were taken from them.) Also, many young children were taken from the fire and baptized against the will of their mothers and fathers. *And all debts owed to the Jews were cancelled, and all the pledges and promissory notes were returned. But the town council took the ready money and possessions they had and distributed them among the craftsmen; but there were many who gave their portion to Our Lady's work or for God's sake.* (For God's sake!) Also, this year, not only the Jews of Strasbourg were burnt, but Jews in all towns along the Rhine. Some towns burnt their Jews after judgment and according to law, others without judgment or law, and in many places the Jews set fire to their own houses and burnt themselves inside.'

cleverer and better ones! In former times we had the better religion, the sole true religion. Now, of course, we don't get so excited about religion; in fact it's not quite so certain any more that our religion is the absolutely true one; indeed, religion in general is no longer absolutely true in that way; we don't hold fast to it any more. Progress! But what we do hold fast to, what we do get excited about in this instance, is the most important fact, beyond all doubt – and this is absolutely true – that we are the better race. We say "better" out of modesty, and in all modesty we go on to say that we alone are the genuinely noble race, the gifted and moral race!'

It is splendid for men in all the world to have Jews, because by this very fact all men everywhere become better people. It is salutary for the world to have this kind of underworld, and a scapegoat responsible for all that makes people discontented. But when and where are people ever content? Never and nowhere. They were not content in paradise, as we can see from the 'fall' of the first human beings. Even the first human beings, in paradise, failed to notice that they were in paradise; there are no paradises, only paradises lost. People are never and nowhere content, not even in heaven, as is clear from Lucifer's rebellion and also – perhaps this God will forgive me all my sins, including the one I am about to commit in writing these things – since God himself was not content in his eternal bliss and repose:otherwise how could he have taken the notion of undertaking such a frantic week's work of creation and bringing about a world of turmoil for the rest of his eternity?

Eternally he cannot forgive himself for this sin of his that lasts for eternity. How splendid to have a scapegoat, whether one is discontented or happy; everything can be loaded on to the scapegoat, all the rage arising from misfortune, and all the wanton arrogance and tomfoolery that comes from good fortune. It is just the same after victory as after having lost a war: the Jews always come in for it, after 1870 just like after 1918. This is how it has always been, and still is.

3.

WHY IS THE JEW A SCAPEGOAT?

Why? Why are the Jews the scapegoats for everyone else?

Anti-Semites only form part of the population; against them there is another segment of the population which is aware of the injustice done to Jews, and aware of it as injustice. And the real anti-Semites, with their explicit injustice and hostility towards Jews, also constitute only a small portion of the population. Equally, however, those who have an interest in the Jews, who display justice and friendship towards them, are only a small part of the population. As we have seen, they are only those who have some interest in associating with Jews, arising from the interest of love, of possession, and of honour-vanity. Without this connection, without their own interest being involved, they would not bestir themselves for justice. That is why it is only the few exceptional people who take any action, people who have not only the thought that arises from interest but also the genuine interest in thought, people who think non-egoistically. But their conviction and the initiatives they take are to no avail among the nonthinking public, i.e., those who have no interest in justice. It is to no avail even though they are supported by those who, from motives of self-interest, are interested in justice for the Jews.

It is to no avail because people at large have no interest in assisting Jews to obtain justice; particularly as they can satisfy their own interest in the achievements of Jews without granting the latter justice. (We shall return to this later.) What could stir them up, what could transform their passivity into activity, but interest? And that is precisely what they lack. They 'do not even think of it' – because they have no interest; and we know that men only think when they are driven to do so by some interest. 'It does not occur to them to bestir themselves' because they do not see that it touches their interest. Who will rouse himself to action over the status quo if it does not make him uncomfortable? Be that as it may, habit obstructs thought. We are so used to antisemitism that we fail to realize what it actually is: antisemitism is hatred of Jews, and hatred of Jews is in turn hatred of mankind. Basically, surely, it cannot be as bad as this – it's only bad for the Jews; we ourselves feel no injustice or pain because of it, not so much as is felt by the tiniest Jewish soul that feels itself to be ill-treated. People actually feel righteous themselves, and very upright and clever people *smile* in the most magnanimous, clever and just way at antisemitism and the Jews. Finally, if

they are pressed, they come out - most justly - with their 'on the
one side' and 'on the other side', whereby, in the end, justice
comes down on the other side - on any side except that of the
Jews. Just as the dot on the 'i' usually falls over some letter
that does not require it, a genuine 'salient point'. Oh, no one
thinks more justly about Jews than they do, but eventually they
come round to it: 'One knows, all the same, that...' - not the
Jews to whom one happens to be speaking, naturally!
Although they dissemble a little and ultimately give themselves
away - for the best actor is still only an actor. Garrick once
said to one of them: 'You played the drunk magnificently; a
pity that his right foot was sober.' And no doubt people are
really convinced: not the Jews to whom one is speaking, and
certainly not all Jews. And yet! They begin by extolling justice
and conclude by defending prejudice. They are tolerant, but in
the end what comes out is hatred, or very close to hatred. And
they do nothing, very definitely, that might offend pride and
hatred, or get in its way.

For in reality 'one' does not think about Jews at all,
either justly or unjustly: 'one' has an interest in being against
them. There may be no open interest against them, but there
is a covert one; they are always seen en bloc as 'the others'.
Anyone who has spun around for long enough in front of
certain objects will see them spinning round even when he has
stopped spinning. The Jew is a Jew, and there is something
despicable about being a Jew. Not for nothing were the Jews
so long despised; lost honour is slow to be restored, and both

individuals and communities experience a difficult recovery; Jews are still despised by many. Despised by the many, it would be hard to say how despised they still are even by those who do not despise them with all their hearts and are by no means convinced that they are wicked. Do people believe, then, only on the basis of conviction and what they can see? We should have little cause to speak of belief if there were not so many who do not see and yet believe, who are not convinced and yet believe; not alone do they believe on the basis of the shakiest conviction: they even believe *contrary* to their conviction: they believe others. Generally, however, men believe themselves rather than others. Only in matters of superstition – and the *Doctrine of the Spiritual Élite and the Multitude* teaches us that moralistic criticism and moralistic pride (which is what we are concerned with here) are part of that superstition that is destructive of life – only in matters of superstition does man believe others rather than himself. He believes that the others have actually seen whatever it is and must be convinced, and so he believes too. In the same way people believe one another with regard to the Jews and despise Jews because others do. The Jews have had it, because, whether they deserve it or not, they do not belong to the society of honourable people. We have spoken of the pride which vaunts itself of its mere membership of the community, without any positive merit, indeed, even where it displays the greatest personal unworthiness. This is particularly so where there is the addition of the weight of inherited prejudice and the word 'Jew.' The word 'Jew' contains within itself the whole evil inheritance; this is where the hatred of Jews lodges. We are entangled in the centuries-old web of suggestion. Generally speaking, what do people know of most things but words and whatever they have heard and believe about such words? They are quicker to believe what they hear than to know what they see.

And as for the word 'Jew', what kind of a word has that become in the world! Language has become a deadly enemy to Jews on account of this word 'Jew'. For it does not simply denote, innocently, the community of those of Jewish descent, or (which would retain a modicum of innocence) the community of 'the others': the word has no trace of innocence left in it, referring as it does, stridently and insistently, to the community of swindlers and deceivers. All others 'others', every other member of a foreign state acquires respect and regard because of the community which stands behind him; the Jew is annihilated by the community into which the word 'Jew' casts him, the community of swindlers and deceivers. We have seen, however, that the idea of a Jewish community of this kind has nothing behind it but the moralistic criticism and slander produced by the antisemitic interest-judgment, which is contrary to the facts and to history, and stands all truth on its head. Anti-Semites claim, falsely, to know the Jews, but in fact they are those who do *not* know Jews and who have an interest or supposed interest in not knowing them and not associating with them. Those who do associate with them, on the basis of lower or higher life-interest, and who really know them, show themselves to be free from prejudice and hatred.

[3]The slander of antisemitic moralistic criticism has completely taken over the word 'Jew', so that it no longer designates the Jewish person. The name 'Jew' which has come down to us is a sediment from the filthiest streams of the middle ages; it has become an antisemitic word, the primal antisemitic word, and has been taken up into the world's evil dictionary, the dictionary of that superstition which causes man to turn in hostility directly against his own kind. The word 'Jew' is now the most disgusting verbal insult in the world, a dangerous, malicious word; it assassinates. It dispatches people at a stroke; like a guillotine, it wipes out the most guiltless and pure from the society of the honourable and dishonourable. The word 'Jew' is even worse than the Jews: it wounds the lips and makes people shudder, even non-anti-Semites who no longer shudder at the physical presence of Jews. Indeed, hundreds of thousands of people know that it is meaningless to feel this way just because

---

[3] This is acknowledged even by erstwhile anti-Semites. Thus, for example, von Gerlach writes: 'To be really immune to antisemitism, one ought really to have known the antisemitic parties from the inside. I speak from experience. As the son of a conservative family I was an anti-Semite in my youth. I attacked the Jews so long as I had no knowledge of them and little more of the leaders of antisemitism. Once I had become personally more acquainted, on the one hand, with men like Charles Hallgarten, Leo Arons, Gustav Landauer, etc., and on the other hand with Liebermann, v. Sonnenberg and his political drinking-companions, I knew where my place was. There is nothing more shallow, unscientific and pharisaical than organized antisemitism. I know only one way of successfully combating antisemitism: political enlightenment. Antisemitism must not be suppressed; it must be spiritually and intellectually overcome - and that does not require a great deal of intellect, only an average measure of political culture. But that is precisely what countless numbers of our 'educated' people lack.'

of a mere word, but they are powerless to extricate themselves from its spell.

There are some who see further than this meaninglessness; they have an idea of the mischievous role moralistic criticism has played in the human community, and that the critics are generally not a whit better than those they criticize, and that hatred is usually to be explained as arising from the nature of the hater rather than the hated. Some even possess the profound insight (expressed in its greatest form by Christ) that men, with their moralistic criticism on which they so pride themselves, shoulder an immense guilt. At least at the level of feelings, however, even people such as these will still tend, with regard to the moralistic criticism applied to Jews, to push the guilt on to the Jews. Inwardly they will not be so very many thousand miles away from the mentality of their contemporaries, and they will incline to regard the injustice meted out to Jews as in some way their punishment. A crude way of thought, like that of Job's friends, who could not distinguish suffering from sin. For many, Job, i.e., 'the persecuted', symbolizes the Jews.

Latent hatred of Jews is still abroad today, and under certain circumstances it can prove dangerous to Jewish people; no doubt those who have so far been quiet will one day howl with the antisemitic wolves–and bite like them. (And *if* the individual's immediate interests are not involved, he will act according to the interest of the group, possibly an inflamed group.) *Could* Jews be in danger under certain circumstances? It is the latent antisemitism in society that forms the real danger to them. It is this society as a whole which perpetrates injustice against Jews, not exclusively those who are called anti-Semites. Anti-Semites cannot be totally separated from the rest of society.

Let us press this inquiry further: how does society stand vis-à-vis antisemitism? Does society really feel antisemitism to be an injustice? Is society ashamed of antisemitism? Is it ashamed of it and disgusted at it enough to take action against it? The question is: does society and the state guarantee an honourable position to Jewish citizens equally, and are they protected against insult and calumny? The question is: since, in this society, the slanderers who want to rob others of their honour become dishonourable themselves, and rightly so (and in former Roman times the only crime rendering a person guilty of infamy was that of *calumnia and praevaricatio*), does this society also strip the antisemitic slanderers of their honour? Or do society and the state tolerate people constantly sowing the dragon's seed of antisemitic slander and inciting others to resentment and persecution of Jews? The question is: what is the judgment of society concerning the antisemitic judgment? Surely, having regard to the facts of its history, its cultural milieu and its practical response to the achievements of living Jews, society's judgment should be totally different from that of the anti-Semites? For a true judgment must base itself solely on the facts. We must press the point, however: how does this society and its judgment stand with regard to the *factual object* of its judgment, and what *is* this judgment?

Answer: it may not be identical with the judgment of antisemitism, but it is very similar to it; it seems as if facts are completely irrelevant to this judgment, just as in the case of interest-judgments. Facts and judgment take no notice of each other. What we see is judgment stubbornly relying on itself alone (flying in the face of all the facts), which serves to promote antisemitism to a position of power and surrounds Jews with danger so that they have no escape. So if we ask what is society's attitude to antisemitism, the answer is this: the danger which hangs immobile over Jews and which falls upon them here, there, today or tomorrow is...society itself. Without society's pride, which is always magnanimously ready to lend a hand, the real anti-Semites with their insane pride would not be such a threat. Jews could deal with anti-Semites on their own. But it is society which is a danger to Jews and, as far as it can, renders them dishonourable.

Naturally, it can only do this to the extent that cultural circumstances permit. Let us be more precise and speak of today's circumstances, so that we may not be accused of making wild assertions, as if nowadays the Jews everywhere were totally dishonourable and outside the laws (which is not borne out by the facts), and so that we may be clear about the fairly obvious fact that Jews are still quite sufficiently dishonoured. (In older German usage, as now, the term *ehrlos*, dishonourable, by no means applied only to those who were totally lacking in honour and legality.) Today Jews are not in a situation of complete dishonour; they have not been totally deprived of their honour (*consumtio famae*), but, unlike others, they exist in a kind of partial dishonour between honour and disgrace, a situation in which their honour is severely diminished (*minutio famae*). At this juncture we need not press the point that, in many respects, they do not even have the benefit of due process of law, practically speaking; this is closely connected to the fact that, while every man has his natural honour, the Jew has his natural dishonour.

Every man has his natural honour and hence his negative free existence, so long as he himself does not diminish it by what he does or allows others to do, or by practising a trade injurious to his honour. He is protected by public conscience and by publicly enforced law against insults and calumnies. Every Jew, however, has his natural dishonour; he lacks negative honour, even if, on the basis of his talents and achievements, he could claim positive honour for himself; he is exposed, defenceless, to insults and slander. True, the honourable Jew will find himself protected if anyone calls him a swindler, but anyone may with impunity call him a Jew. And since 'Jew' means 'crook' and everything that is bad (which is why the word is applied to non-Jews as a way of branding them), it follows that anyone may call the honourable Jew a swindler, etc. and trample on him, and get away with it. It would be worthy of serious consideration whether the word 'Jew', employed with *animus iniurandi*, should not be included among the insults punishable by law. For it is pure sophistry to say that the word 'Jew' is no more an insult than the word 'German' or 'Celt'; unlike these names, it is in fact used as an insult. Similarly, the common practice of insulting and slandering Jews should be punished. If men are not just unless it brings them some advantage, they will be less unjust if injustice brings some disadvantage upon them. (Fear cures many an illness and the police make more blind men to see and lame men to walk than Christ did.) So it would be beneficial if there were a law against insulting and slandering Jews, punishable, for instance, by the withdrawal of political suffrage for a period. Would this not be creating an exception in law, since insults and calumnies are not generally actionable? But the Jewish question is itself an exceptional case, and the insults and calumnies, while they are general and common, definitely affect individuals and result in practical disadvantage to them. Everyone has law on his side against the unlawful expression of contempt, except the Jew. This is his punishment for being born a Jew, a punishment without either justice or purpose; for only he ought to be punished who has culpably given some hurt to another; he who is not culpable should not be punished either. This is wanton punishment, where there is no relation to guilt. For in by far the most cases the people thus punished are quite innocent. It improves nothing, for those who suffer this punishment are only human beings with their ordinary human nature; no one can expect any other person to get beyond his own nature. This punishment is really and truly culpable itself.

Forgive me, gentle reader, for putting forward such trivialities without any apology! And there are other readers to whom I owe, not an apology for uttering platitudes, but rather a defence for having put forward monstrous notions to people to whom the very opposite is only common sense. Who will say that what I have said here is a self-evident truth? But even if the rights of the Jew constitute a self-evident triviality, I would still like to repeat this triviality unwearyingly so long as antisemitism is also a triviality, so long as the triviality of the law does not apply to Jews. What advantage is it to truth to have become trivial, if untruth and injustice are practised? Writers who are concerned for more than novelties in a witty and glittering game – such writers must be really trivial and strange if they are to write about the two trivialities which are locked in shameful combat, if they are to speak of such things and bring to people's awareness and consciences the fact that the law is not so self-evident and obvious where Jews are concerned. Serious writers must continually write this: the Jew, who has incurred no guilt that would need to be expiated by him, who has committed no contemptible act and carries out no contemptible trade, is yet automatically tainted, like someone punished by law; something contemptible (*turpitudo*) clings to him. The name 'Jew' attracts invective, makes him a *persona turpis, infamis.* By birth every man has his legal status and his natural honour, but every Jew has his inherited injustice and his natural dishonour. That is something taken for granted by the law, a triviality. This shows us the Jew's special relationship to honour and dishonour; it shows us what has been taken from him.

To take the honour from a human being – mentioning
this is also a triviality, yet necessary in order to make it
thoroughly clear to people (as I have done before) what Jews
suffer, and why – to take the honour from a human being is to
take away his personality and his life's freedom. The whole
sphere of those with whom he lives, the whole of society must
be the sphere of his freedom and peace. No man's honour
should be slighted without his having merited it, and no
guiltless man's honour should be touched with impunity. And
what applies to men must also apply to Jews – yes or no? No.
It does not apply to Jews: society cheats them of their honour,
of their positive honour and their negative honour, their
membership of society; it remains in its pride, representing the
deception it practises as a punishment for the guilt of Jews.

4.

A MAN FROM ANOTHER PLANET WONDERS...

Any impartial person who learns, sees or hears of this injustice, this monstrous violation, and has not had the word 'Jew' constantly dinned into his ears on all occasions, as is usual among us, is bound to be utterly appalled at it. Let us imagine that some being related to man were to come to our earth from another planet to study our human history and the conditions which prevail in our human community. What questions might this being ask?

'What are you doing with the Jews? Are not Jews human beings just like non-Jews? Are their achievements not like yours? I can see no difference, and you yourselves seem to make none. You go to Jewish merchants just as to non-Jewish ones, you read books written by Jews, you employ Jewish lawyers to deal with your most important affairs, you entrust your lives to Jewish physicians; doubtless you place an equal trust in the capability and conscientiousness of Jews as of non-Jews, and make no distinction between them. And yet that does not stop you making distinctions in assessing them socially: at that level Jews are by no means equal to non-Jews. Observing the manner and basis of your life and society, where, it seems, people are assessed solely according to their conscientiousness and achievements, and honour is just as essential to life as property, and where social standing is part of the reward for achievement, it strikes me most forcibly that you give Jews only money, but no honour.

Thus you only pay them the half of what they are owed – and
for achievements you yourselves recognize as full
achievements. For by making use of them just as you make use
of the services of non-Jews (whom you recompense not only
with money but also with honours), you acknowledge the full
value of what Jews produce while only paying them half the
rate.

What? 'Simply because they are Jews?'

I see. "Jews" means "inferior human beings?"
Does that mean "people who have no need of honour?" Are
Jews human beings who assert that they need no honour? Jews
do not apparently deviate from the human species in this way.
I discern in human beings an instinct for honour that is almost
as strong as the instinct of self-preservation and self-
sustenance. Jews' hearts, too, are full of the longing for
honour: they long for it as their natural right and property,
which you are denying them.

Oh? You *do not need* to give them any honour because
they are deviants from the human species and are worse than
you are? But are they really worse? I cannot see that they are
either cleverer or more stupid than you, as to what you call
good or bad; nor do they seem any worse or better. What do
you mean with your "good" and "bad"? It is by no means so
easy to say which of you is "good" or "bad," or even if there is a
single good person among you. It seems to me that those
among you who bear the worst name are not as bad as their
name; and no one, however glorious his name, is as good as his
name. Which of you is good? What does the Jew say?

"No one is good but God alone!" But if really no one is good, no one is better, either.

You with your "better than others"! Do you still have so little self-knowledge? Do you not know that, among you, it is those who are stronger who call themselves "better", and that, likewise, those who are weaker call themselves "better"? You who are "good" are not good: you are rich and strong; and you who are "bad" are not bad: you are weak. The strong ones who call themselves better have a stronger case than the weak and better ones inasmuch as they are stronger. That is how it has always been among you, and still is. Black men and Armenians are bad, too, because they are few in number and the weak ones in your midst; for I cannot see that they are any worse than you are, just as I cannot see it in the case of the Jews. It reminds me of the story of the sick man whose body was examined after his death and revealed all the signs, in the most precise detail, that the doctors had predicted: if there were such indicators for wickedness, they would probably be found on examining an average Jew. But it also seems probable to me that it might be like the case of the autopsy performed by mistake on the wrong person; thus the signs of wickedness might be found on an average non-Jew just as likely as on the average Jew.

What are you doing with the Jews? Surely you cannot believe that they really are all bad? You cannot believe this any more than you can still believe in stories of witches and ghosts. How many, then, are supposed to be

"bad"? Half? A quarter? A tenth? Or just a few more than
are "bad" among you? There is scarcely any one among you
who is really "bad", totally black; just as there is no one totally
white. (Indeed, none of you is white or black; you are all
grey—with all your black-and-white talk!) You human beings
are only really bad, so to speak, by way of exception, but in the
case of the Jews you make the exception the rule and say that
the Jewish race is bad. Compared with this, even the "eye for
an eye and tooth for a tooth" is reasonable. How bad your
deeds show you to be! You make the entire Jewish race atone
because of a few bad Jews!

For myself, I cannot see things as you do; I do not see
you as human beings and Jews as Jews: to me, Jews are human
beings like you. I am simply amazed at so much of what is said
about the Jews and that you are prepared to believe. But I
suppose you must have unbelievable things to believe, and the
more the merrier; that is your number one preoccupation,
continually hoaxing one another; and that in itself causes truth
always to come to grief where you are concerned and prevents
it from introducing light into your souls. As for me, I cannot
see any difference between Jews and yourselves; and if you
were able to see, you would see both defects and virtues in
Jews. I know of frightful defects in Jews, but I will say nothing
evil about Jews, for you say too much evil about them. So I will
not talk about their defects, but only add what you yourselves
always forget to add, namely, that the Jews' failings are human
failings.

Do you not recognize the human failings of one another? Has one of your painters ever lacked scoundrels to be depicted in his scenes of hell or drowned in the Flood? Do I have to remind you how your nations think of each other and deal with each other once they have the power to do so? Don't they treat each other in a very Jewish manner! But you only have to look at your own experience of life with those closest to you, at how you act and get along with one another in your families, your brothers and sisters and even your parents and children: do you not make each other spend the entire day holding your breath? Do you not make yourselves thoroughly unhappy because of your failings? And on the other hand, do you find any greater happiness than in acknowledging people's virtues in your mind and heart and in being able to love those who excel? The virtues of Jews, however, and Jews who excel do not make you happier and cheerful; you translate their virtues into vices, and there is not one man among you who hesitates to condemn Jews on account of defects he himself possesses. He should even be slow to condemn them for faults he himself does not possess – because he assuredly has other faults of equal moment to take their place. You human beings are recognizable as such by your failings just as surely as by your thoughts and your appearance; so, too, you recognize human failings in one another and assuredly are quick to point them out. But where Jews are concerned you point the finger at *all Jews*; where Jews are concerned your humane perspective stops and your perspective on Jews takes over. Once you

come to Jews you suddenly recognize, without the least
uneasiness and from a position of superiority, that human
defects only occur in Jews; you even try to wipe off your filth
and ill-temper on them, as if it came from them in the first
place. Oh what angels of light you would be but for these
mischievous seducers!

 Would you really? Were you any better in the "good
old days" when you were able to keep Jews in the ghetto?
Were you any less slaves of Mammon?[1] You act as if the sin of
your world had only entered into the Jews.

---

[1] As for 'the good old days', the speaker from the other planet is right, and
V. A. Huber is right when he says that human vices have also been essentially
the same in all ages and that 'the good old days' simply never existed. (V. A.
Hubers Ausgewählte Schriften, ed. K. Munding, Berlin, Aktiengesellschaft
Pionier, p. 431ff: Die gute alte Zeit: 'As regards Mammonism in particular,
it would take us too far if we were to examine in any detail, for instance, the
effects of American silver and gold on 16th century conditions – a
characteristic of the "financiers" of olden times, who enjoyed the same ill-
repute as today's stock market men. For our purposes it will suffice merely
to mention the two most famous frauds of history, that of Law in France and
the so-called "South Sea bubble" in England. Going further back into the
middle ages, the picture which Dante paints, as with a red-hot iron, of the
Florence of his times, shows more or less all the traits attributed to our own
day as consequences of Mammonism, etc. Here we are not concerned with
the question of how far the magnificent depiction of "old Florence" presented
by the great, stern poet and statesman (who is impartial in the highest
meaning of the word) would survive a searching historical critique – if we had
detailed documents from those times. Nor do we lack examples, from other
areas, of this kind of bright vein of silver between antecedent and subsequent
darkness, be it the darkness of savagery or of corruption. Practically all these
testimonies from the past (leaving aside the actual satirists) refer, as is to be
expected, more or less to the extreme phenomena and the curious features of
a given period or locality. No further proof is needed, however, that these
extremes point to a certain universality, or at least a breadth, or more or less
tempered effects of the same causes, e.g., covetousness, ambition, sensuality,
ostentation, pride, etc.', idem on p. 448.

That is no less absurd than if you wanted to say that only Jews become sick and die, whereas in fact they lived longer than you do. You call human defects Jewish defects, and thus you call the Jews bad and hate them for it. Indeed, this is how it is: what you call the Jews' badness is in fact your own faults. You need to know that someone is a Jew first before you can find and hate the Jewish badness in him. But you are no better for thinking yourselves to be better; this I know, for I can compare the true human plant which you really are with the bloated self-deception of the men you imagine yourselves to be. I – who do not have your perspective on Jews – I cannot see that the Jews are worse.

It is a wonder that they do not treat you worse and stir up more evil:

> The man who sees his rights by others stolen
> Is justified in his own eyes in treating others so.
> But given and made to feel himself a human being
> He'll never seek mankind to undermine or overthrow.

The Jews, however, seem totally incapable of being worse than you are. Even where they are most oppressed by you, Jews are no worse than you; they are certainly not inwardly humiliated, they are neither spiritually nor morally degenerate (since there is not a single Jew to be found among the names of the worst criminals and monsters preserved in your tradition); nor is it true that their best qualities have broken faith with them and gone over to your side. And if you say they are worse because they are Jews – and you are no better than the Jews – you are actually saying that the Jews do not need to be worse per se: the fact that they are called Jews makes them worse. I simply do not understand how anyone can be bad just because of a name they bear. (Of course we are not talking about the name "Jew", but about Jews; you cannot pretend that "Jews" are only a word and that their human nature is merely amorphous and secondary.) I do not understand how human beings on whom you place reliance – and you do, since Jewish businessmen, doctors, lawyers, artists, scholars, writers, journalists, etc., pursue their professions not only for Jews: they operate equally well for you and are engaged by you; indeed, you evidently give pride of place to Jewish merchants, doctors and lawyers, otherwise there would not be so many more of them than their proportion of the population would lead one to expect. Not to mention the Jewish contribution to journalism related to art and literature: only an insignificant minority of those interested in art and literature reads anything but "the Jewish press." – I do not understand how people can acknowledge, in practice, the full value of others' achievements while at the same time rendering them inferior on account of a mere name. It is beyond my comprehension; there must be earthly words whose meaning and significance I cannot penetrate. After all, the word "Jew" is only a word, only a name like other names, bearing no more similarity to Jews than other names to what they denominate; it is nothing in itself, it does not change anything in the human beings who bear this name, neither adding to them nor taking away from them. But why, in any case? What makes you apply, to people to whom you owe both money and honour, a name which apparently suggests to you that those who bear it are guilty of deceit? You would be better than you are if you lacked the power to speak and give names to others! And why use this miracle-working name to deprive Jews only of their honour? Why not deprive them of their money too?...Off with you, you are trying to make a fool of me. Yet you are far from fooling when it comes to names. For instance, any of you could be called murderers, e.g., those with light blue eyes, those called Schultz and Müller, and those with a "von" in their surname; they could all be taken into custody and brought to the place of execution. Of course they are not murderers, but so what? They have been called "murderers" and the name is enough. At least the word "murderer" denotes something really wicked. But "Jews" only refers to their origin – and you all have origins too, even if, unlike the Jews, you are not so sure what they are. Is it dishonouring for the Jews to be able to trace their descent far back, whereas for you it would be honourable? The name "Jew" only refers to descent and means literally, in Hebrew, nothing other than "those pledged to God". If you translate it differently and say it means that you do not need to give Jews what is their right, it would be better

to give them a different name immediately so that you can give
them what is due to them.

I do not understand you at all.   The Jews are
industrious, and you are absurd. When I see how you treat the
Jews (and you do not treat them well, at any rate), and how you
call them worse and morally inferior human beings in spite of
their industriousness and the important role they have played
in your history, it seems to me that what you are doing to the
Jews is something inferior and even odious; on this account you
could be denied *your* honour, particularly since you pride
yourselves on this hateful and disgraceful conduct of yours.
You are blind or malicious if you say that Jews in general are
less gifted and morally more unworthy, going on to inflict
suffering on those whom you have already made to suffer so
much and to whom you owe so many thanks. Not surprisingly,
it is precisely those among you who would most need to reflect
upon their intellectual and spiritual endowments and their own
moral behaviour, those who are the most blind and malicious,
the morally most corrupt and filthy, who are most zealous in
flinging mud at the Jews. Indeed, I understand less and less,
the more I reflect on the fact that the Jews form the most
important source for the mainstream of your history, and that
those you call morally inferior have exercised by far the
strongest ethical influence upon you. I do not mean by this
that they made you better; I am speaking of the facts of your
history and civilization and echoing your own dictum.

According to this one dictum of yours you have received your best ethical principles from the hands of Jews; do you say this by way of demonstrating the truth of your other dictum regarding the ethical inferiority of the Jewish race? First you would have to demonstrate, by means of similar achievements, that your race is ethically equal, that you could genuinely do without Jews and do not need to go to these ethically unworthy beings for products of the heart – for they who can speak so well from the heart must actually *have* hearts. Be serious: prove your ethical equality by showing your ethically equivalent achievements; in fact, since you call yourselves ethically better, you should even have ethically better achievements, but I will only ask for equivalent ones. No doubt you have a great many? For there are many of you, and the Jews are few in number. Now, where are they? Let's see them, all these many achievements! Or even if there's only one, let's see it! The audience is silent, says nothing – you seem better at proving that Jews are bad than that you are good and better; even what you call your best is the achievement of the "bad" Jews. There is something very wrong here: there is something wanton, corrupt and incurable in you, for you cannot speak of these things except with a false tongue that gives the lie to itself. For if you, the many, the better ones, have little to show, if you do not have a single thing that is better, not even a single thing of equal value; if you are obliged to admit that, of all the most influential achievements among

you, the most influential, the best and first come from
Jews – this is like a thunderclap of judgment, rejecting what you
who are more numerous and better say about the Jews, i.e.,
that they are the worst and last among you.

I do not know whether I have spoken clearly enough to
make you understand the way you are. Why you are like this is
more than I can comprehend. Recently I read some
illuminating words concerning the Jews' significance for your
history and civilization in Constantin Brunner, in the last part
of his book, *Der Judenhass und die Juden.* You should read it.
What do you do? This is the most astounding thing of all I
have seen during my stay among you: this monstrous
distinction you draw so sharply and ruthlessly, the distinction
between what is Jewish and the Jew. What do you do? You
make what is Jewish your prime achievement and set the Jew
on the lowest place; the wolf prays the "Our Father" while
snapping at the sheep which taught it to him. The idea keeps
coming back to me, more and more puzzling, and there is no
answer to it: what kind of logic is it in your judgment that
connects what you hold to be the first, what is dearest to you
and most admired, namely, Judaism (or Christianity, as you call
it), with what you regard as the last and least, namely, the
despised, hated and abhorred Jew? For in reality the two are
bound up with each other. For Judaism or Christianity is a
product of Jews, a product of the Jewish race. Judaism or
Christianity or, to speak more correctly, the Bible, is a product
of the Jewish race.

And of this Bible I tell you–and the best of you will have to agree with me–that it is the best of all that your mankind has produced; thus the Jewish race has produced the best and most powerful thing in mankind. And if there is anything of yours, of your period of mankind's history, that is likely to survive to some other historical period of your human race, irrespective of changes in the world, it seems to me that the Bible has the best prospects, this timeless, eternal Bible, which has its roots in the nature of man and knows man in his heights and his depths.

What kind of reasoning is yours, which requires the idea of the Jewish race being worse and less gifted to excite it? Both the Bible and Christ pledge their renown on you being wrong. Why is it that, out of all the Jewish race, you only see those who are bad? You see those who are neither good nor bad as simply bad; you even see the best as bad, and yourselves as the better ones. You would be better if you prided yourselves less on being better. If it is true that there are more of the worse sort among the Jews than there should be according to their proportion of the population, we need to look and see whether the converse might also be true, i.e., that there is among Jews a greater proportion of the better sort, too, than among the rest of the population. If so, perhaps the Jews must be regarded as the strongest in all that is human, in good as in evil; but this would still not make them worse and you better. Never forget, therefore, that your best, your most

potent achievement is due to the Jewish race, and that in your
society of the better and stronger, in the very place you have
left for the one who is best and strongest, there sits, by your
own appointment – a Jew.

You should give genuine *thought* to Jews, rather than
circling round them with your contradictions, torn between
admiration for what is Jewish and contempt for Jews
themselves.   Will you not drop the rigid inanity of this
reciprocal conventional babbling and start thinking? But if you
cannot, and can only go on putting questions the way you
do – and I have already said that I can see no difference
between you and the Jews: I see nothing but human beings – if
you cannot do anything else but keep asking whether Jews are
not worse and less gifted human beings, I am bound to tell you
that you could with equal justification turn the question round:
you could just as well ask whether Jews are not more gifted and
better human beings. And I advise those of you who are Jews,
when you ask about their lack of gifts and badness of character,
to put another question in return: ask whether Judaism is not
the most noble and strongest element in our culture. They may
have a small opinion of themselves, but they cannot think
highly enough of Judaism. Where do you get this notion that
the Jewish race is in league with evil powers? – for it causes you
to deny normal social respect to these Jews, one of whom
you yourselves call the greatest honour of your entire
human race.   Indeed, without this man your humanity –

with all the men you can present–would possess far less real honour.'

This is Constantin Brunner's reply to his reader from another planet: society denies Jews their due honour because the Jews achieve the same without this honour as with it. This is taken care of by the Jews' urge to live and the urge to pursue the ideal. For its part, society only needs to pay money, not money and honour. Society only pays what it has to, it buys as advantageously as it can, even if the seller comes to harm as a result. That is not enough to prove it inferior; nor is it inferior on account of the contradictions between its practice and its judgments and because it calumniates those with whom it has sat down to eat. Gentle reader from another planet, on our planet such uncovering of contradictions has no effect whatsoever, for our whole society, all human society, is like this; it cannot be termed inferior, because it is the same in all places, always has been, and looks as if it will remain so for the future. Nor do we scratch our heads (which in these present ages of mankind expresses puzzlement) or spend a long time brooding and wondering how, in a situation of contradiction and dishonesty, we can act with real integrity; we just get on with it. We call this 'Columbus's egg'; it is a source of much admiration and amusement. As for the principles of thought of honesty and justice, I do not know whether they are in common use among you, and what, in your case, takes the place of social esteem: among us, in general, decisions are not taken on the basis of thought or justice, but each one has his interest and power, or his interest and his lack of power, and his honour or dishonour in society follows from this.

The very isolated few who have real thought and real justice are obliged to take these two things and go and dwell in hiding on the outermost margins of life. There, indeed, they can be *blessed* in themselves, in their authentic, eternal Self, knowing that they are miraculously one with all mankind's great men, with all who love. But they can never achieve a genuinely happy life together with the others, and may not show themselves publicly with their thought and their justice, otherwise they would be the butt of mockery and ill-treatment. That is how powerless they are over against the generality of men; they are totally unable to restrain and guide those whom they cannot teach – for while man is an animal that can be led astray [verführbar], he cannot be led [führen] by reason. True, justice can of course be obtained at the hands of judges, but there is no such thing as a proper rule of justice. For judges are not involved with the great concerns of injustice which are invisible to ordinary eyes, and which show that ordinary people have an interest in injustice. Judges are concerned to see that the small issues of injustice are carried out with the appearance of legality; they can judge these small issues disinterestedly and justly – but that is still not justice. There really is no spot   on   earth   where   justice   can   freely   operate!

It is the power behind the judges that decides the outcome, and all resistance to it is hopeless. The fact that the judges consistently decide so justly and piously is due to a highly remarkable, cunning ploy: they are paid to have an interest in justice. Just as attorneys are nourished by injustices, judges live by justice – naturally only by justice in other people's affairs; they are just because they get money for it. As soon as men have an interest in promoting justice, therefore, and the power to do so, they do actually promote it; just as they act unjustly once their interest requires it and their power makes it possible.

Where the generality is concerned, with its great injustice towards Jews, the situation is hopeless. Jews have no prospect of successful litigation, against the generality of men, before a judge such as this: 'And righteousness shall be the girdle of his loins, and faithfulness the girdle of his reins.' The generality of men is engaged in power struggle against Jews and itself plays the part of judge; how could their power fail to win? Their interest and power are opposed to the Jews, and in their injustice, moreover, they think themselves better than Jews. Those with power, the victors, are eternally the better ones, and the vanquished and powerless are eternally the less good. Jews, eternally the losers, must just accept the way society treats them and the way it gets better and richer in terms of honour by giving Jews only money instead of money and honour. The honour it denies to Jews, or the contempt it pours on them, accrues to its own greater honour, the honour of non-Jewish society; it bolsters its sense of itself, its pride and arrogance. It may not be the loud and insolent arrogance of the real anti-Semites, but a quiet pride is pride all the same; and this pride (we repeat), the first of the Seven Deadly Sins, courses in the blood of the entire human race: it is man's pride that rises up against his own kind and against those who are different.

The latent, quiet pride that rises up against Jews is still with us just as much as the open variety. Apart from the presence of admittedly larger groups of non-Jews who are linked with Jews by common interests of love, possession and honour – and we do not wish to underestimate the importance this has and the advance it signifies over earlier conditions – apart from this, compared with the ages of religious suppression, not a great deal has changed. What, in earlier times, was achieved by Christian theologians, stirring up the people and inciting them against Jews because they did not adhere to the Christian religion, is now achieved by the anti-Semites with their racial theories, because the Jews do not belong to that race to which the Anti-Semites – and those whom they address their appeal – supposedly belong. Ordinary people, by nature peaceful, can be stirred up by the vociferous priests of racial hatred just as much as by the loud-mouthed priests of religious hatred, because they have no interest in favour of Jews; in fact they always have a latent interest against Jews.

The world's practice and mode of proceeding against Jews has always been essentially the same. Both socially and historically Jews are cheated of thanks, honour and recognition.   Historically they would deserve the greatest renown for the greatest historical achievement: they have put our world on a new foundation, on which it still stands today. But now, instead of saying that the world has become Jewish, people say that the world has become Christian, and ultimately 'Christian' signifies the inwardly and outwardly hostile opposite of 'Jewish'. This view of things propagates itself automatically by the invisible power of the liar, history, until eventually the facts themselves are stood on their head.   The very *word* 'Christianity' is enough, it does practically everything – again we see that a word can do so much, can do almost anything. Christianity, that is, as a name of respectability, not as a proper name; it would be fatal to use its proper name. For its proper name would be, of course, 'Josephsonism'.   But Christianity sounds better, doesn't it, than Josephsonism?   Far more Christian. And the deception is so *learned*: the respectable name comes, by a roundabout route, from the Greek; Christos is the Greek translation of *Maschiach*. How splendidly remote Christianity sounds from Josephsonism, Messianism and Judaism!   Who, hearing 'Christianity', thinks of Judaism, except in the sense of its despised opposite? This is a victory celebrated with full musical honours. No one is aware any more that Christianity is Judaism baptized, Judaism with a non-Jewish name. Least of all do the Jews themselves know that Christianity was one of the movements within Judaism, at the very core of Judaism, of prophetic Judaism, which failed, however, to embrace and inspire the whole of Jewry. Just as Protestantism failed to embrace and inspire the whole of Christendom. Christianity would not have become the child estranged from and hostile to its mother's womb, and Christ would have spread forth his influence among his own 'if ill-fortune had left sufficient time, if there had not been so few years, years of hardship and war, leading to political annihilation. The dissolution of the Jewish nation, and principally *you* yourselves, have wrenched Christ from his own sphere and cut off his continued influence on Judaism; you have made us hate him. You have made his name a horror to us, you have turned our own blood against us as a scourge; you have obliged us to see Christ in an alien, hostile perspective, from the point view of your Christianity' [*Der Judenhass und die Juden* pp. 358, 359 cf. bibliography]. People have fought the Jews with their own weapons, with none other than Jewish weapons, and no other combatants than Jews. There was not a single non-Jew among the writers of the New Testament, and no one who wanted to be anything other than a Jew. The world talks so much about what Christ suffered for man's sake, and that he took human suffering upon himself out of love; but as for all the Jews have suffered for Christ's sake, and how the Jews had to bear more suffering than all other people, and how through the Jew, Christ, who 'redeemed' all men, the Jews were plunged into damnation – the world says nothing of this.

The world has fought the Jews with Jewish weapons that were no longer called Jewish and using Jews who were no longer called Jews. Enough – yet no, it is not enough; we must say it again: it all rests on the remarks already mentioned in that final section of *Der Judenhass und die Juden* [ibid], where we see how Christ is the most Jewish of all Jews, Christianity is really nothing but Judaism, and how the world has dealt with Jews having become Jewish in its own way: "There is not a single human being in our lands, however poor in ideas, who has not heard, as something fundamental and of prime importance, of the greatness of the Jews, and also of their baseness. There is not a single person who has not been taught to attribute dishonour to them, but also to grant them an honour far outweighing this dishonour. We are well acquainted with the way they contrived to assert both things at once, making strange distinctions and dichotomies. They apportioned honour to what was Jewish but was no longer called Jewish, and to the Jew who was no longer called a Jew; dishonour was allotted to the despoiled Jews, who continued to be called Jews because they refused to accept the expanded form in which the spiritual goods stolen from them had been imitated, and because, by so damnably and stupidly remaining alive (in spite of the efforts made to get rid of them), by simply existing, they were an irrefutable refutation of the

alien imitation. Yes indeed: if they had died out, so that the
legacy of the Jewish spirit could have been freely used, the
Jews would have been laid in the tomb with honour; as
Augustine wrote: *oportuit Synagogam cum honore sepelire.*[*] Or
if they had remained in their land of origin, so that we could
have Judaism sent to us like oranges and bananas! But instead
they themselves came everywhere; they were to be found
everywhere, nasty and strange, spectral. Were we not obliged
to ascribe the Jewish spirit to the Jews?! But was it possible to
ascribe the Jewish spirit to this Jewish spectre?! They did not
exist, and yet, unaccountably, they had an effect; their existence
was hollow, lacking in spirit like a ghost, assuredly lacking in
spirit; for the Christians had the Jewish spirit in the bag. Snip,
snap, and the Christians had plucked the Jewish soul from its
dwelling place and adopted it themselves. So people went on
stigmatizing Judaism on the one hand and divinizing it on the
other, without even suspecting that what they were cutting to
pieces in their minds was, in reality, One. People saw in Jesus
Christ both the humiliation *and* the exaltation (*status
exinanitionis and status exaltationis*), but they did not see that
Jesus Christ belonged to the Jews. For, with regard to the
Jews, people only saw their humiliation; they did not see that,
in this humiliation, the Jews had remained faithful to their lofty
calling. People failed to see the truth uttered by John: 'As he
is, so are we in this world'...In order to get round the Jewish

---

[*] One should bury the Synagogue with honour.

nature of Christianity, people have used (and still use) distortion, falsifications and the most childish of fables, representing Christianity as something that stands entirely on its own feet, something brand new, come straight down from heaven.   The fact that it was fabricated within Judaism is treated as pure chance; it must be squeezed and wrenched from Judaism" [ibid].   This view governs the world of painting, and it is found at the lowest level, in antisemitism with its racial theories.   Painting – rejoice, O Christendom! – has completely un-Jewed and un-Jewished Christ and his disciples, making an exception, with naive spitefulness, of the traitor, Judas.   And the learned propagators of racial hatred – rejoice even more, O Christendom! – have managed to do what painting could not achieve: they have shown that Christ was the opposite of a Jew, namely, a Saxon anti-Semite!

The fame of Christ cannot be done away with.   The fact that he was a phenomenon of world proportions, so serious and noble, so great and free – this could have been undermined by means of slander; ultimately it would have been enough merely to say, 'Jew!'   But who can obscure the fact that this Jew's fame is unique?   Whose fame can compare with his?   And that there is to be no end to it?   Those who have disposed of him as God have only started to deal with him as man all over again.   All have to come to grips with him, even the Jews and the Gentiles for whom, up to now, he has been a stumbling block and foolishness.   He will not let go of individual souls, nor of art, nor of philosophy and mysticism – and all this is supposed to have been engineered by one of those disreputable Jews, someone who not only walks about quite freely in the world, a Jew who is not disreputable but is actually the most honoured of men, our sole really great man, compared with whom the great men among us (who are more gifted and ethically superior) are less gifted and ethically less worthy?! The only thing to be done, as far as possible, is to get rid of the idea that this Jew is a Jew.

The fact that Christ was a Jew and that Christianity is Judaism has been removed from men's awareness; it has been filched and falsified. The great book of mankind has an index of facts, containing references to the gigantic deeds of Jews, but in the other index, the index of persons, their persons are maligned as hideous dwarfs; those who cannot be reviled are given pseudonyms making them unrecognizable as Jews, and there is no reference to the other index where their deeds are highlighted; there is a conspiracy of silence, evasion, trickery, lying, erasures, and the deception is complete. History is falsified, thoughts are falsified, words are falsified; now every word is in itself a falsified thought, a piece of falsified history.

Now that I, who have seen the unsullied truth, have come to show it, they still refuse to look through the instrument by which it can be seen because they have an interest in not seeing it. History takes the Jews' achievement and uses it, but it cheats them of their due renown. This is no crude and ordinary deception: it is a really delicate and extremely mean deception – if I were an anti-Semite and it did not go against the Jews, I would speak of *history's Jewish cunning* which has swindled the Jews. But now I am speaking only of the falsification of history in the interest of pride, this so cunningly devised deception. History goes on, and society is history in its forward movement; it keeps on sewing with the thread cunningly threaded. By now society no longer needs to proceed so artfully; it can quite openly and brutally appropriate the achievements of living Jews and cheat them of their honour.

Society has been doing this to Jews for two thousand years and continues to do so because it had and has the requisite interest and power. This is no exaggeration: this society continues to treat Jews as it has done; just as it has treated Christianity too. Pride, pride, and monstrous falsification in the interest of pride! Christianity is represented as a matter for Christians, for non-Jews; the Christians have taken it over as their glory, and the Jews must wear opprobrium around their necks. Christianity is ours, the Christians' glory; up with the banner of the Cross, and filth and ignominy to the Jews! This society, instead of giving Jews the revenue of renown, robs them of their capital, their heart, their character, their honour. When the Jews are told that Christianity does not belong to them, they are Jews no longer; they are Jews with their miserable Judaism, lacking the spiritual character of Judaism.

For Christianity is not the Christian religion and this Christian society, which acts so unchristianly towards Jews, but the Christianity of Christ, the genial, prophetic Judaism with Christ as its peak. Deprived of honour, Jews are not human beings, at least according to the norm of the society which thus deprives them. The Jews have failed to convert this society to the Christianity of Christ, i.e., to prophetic Judaism; on the contrary, it has even become antisemitic. It could never implement prophetic Judaism.[2] For two thousand years this Christian society, nourished from the roots of Jewish culture, has done to Jews what it accused them of doing; for naturally, the sheep and the rabbit are to blame: the sheep muddied the wolf's water and the rabbit attacked the dog. It has been the same old tune for two thousand years, and for two thousand years this society has prejudged, exploited, suppressed, despicably slandered and sullied Jews.

---

[2] This could not be implemented by any society, for it is genius and spirit, i.e., its nature is to go beyond reality. The significance of this is treated in more detail in my work on Christ [cf. bibliography]. It is ridiculous and depressing that all want to be *Christians*, that is, Christs; it is even more depressing and ridiculous than if all wanted to be Shakespeares and Michelangelos, since Christ is even more of a genius than Shakespeare and Michelangelo. The genial or spiritual nature of Christianity or prophetic Judaism cannot be realized in any unspiritual community; albeit the unspiritual community stands in a relationship of imitation towards all that is brought forth by the spirit. But the unspiritual community imitates the spiritual with its unspiritual consciousness which is specifically different from the spiritual. And in fact, for two thousand years our society, with all its life, with all its life-oriented culture, has been in a relationship of imitation towards this incomparably most powerful spiritual product, the genius of prophetic Judaism.

As we know, human society is constantly full of injustice, but I have searched its history in vain to find a single injustice that is anywhere near as grave and significant as this, that has been committed against Jews for two thousand years and is still being perpetrated entirely without scruple. No other injustice approaches it, either in length of duration or in significance, considering the gravity of the injustice itself as well as the dignity of those against whom it is committed. Nowhere else are the victim's innocence, and the obligations which should be due to him, attested and demonstrated, as here, by the perpetrator himself, by this society.

I am speaking here always of society at large, for those who, in private, give Jews their due social honour are not relevant: there are only a few who are directly interested in the Jews. (And here I am referring only to those who are very directly interested, not even the circles in which one can meet with a good measure of such interest, e.g., not the nobility in general, which has plenty of Jewish blood intermixed in it, but just the interested individuals among the nobility.) Only a few thinking people are really ashamed of themselves, as Prince Hermann von Pückler-Muskau [1785-1871] remarked, for instance: 'Since attaining reason, I am ashamed in the presence of every educated Jew'; or like Magdalena Kasch who, because of her sense of shame, her disgust and the pressure of her conscience regarding the vile

treatment of human beings with Jewish names, wishes to call
herself Cohn. Society makes it so that, in general, Jews have to
live as in an antisemitic community; society is guilty of
antisemitism – 'anti-Semites' are simply those who are carriers
of the latent anti-Jewish attitude (while not being interested in
it themselves; rabid hatred utters its speech within them and
they arouse it in others as soon as some interest or supposed
interest shows itself, whether it be the prospect of humiliating
Jews and the opportunity to satisfy the lust for revenge, which
is sweet even when taken on the innocent; the anti-Semites
summon up the demon of pride in all the others. This is the
pride of society; pride, pride, pride and the falsification of the
facts in the interests of pride. Pride and what follows from it is
not simply the readiness to allow things: it is the positive will
and character of this society of honourable people. Everyone
who belongs to this society stinks of pride against Jews, he is a
scorner, hater, oppressor, tormentor, persecutor of Jews. He is
a slanderer, one who annihilates the honour of others; he
knows well how the slanderer is regarded, and the one who
listens to him: the slanderer has the devil on his tongue and
the one who listens to him has the devil in his ears. How right
it is that men could find no worse word for the devil than this
very word, devil, $\delta\iota\alpha\beta o\lambda o\varsigma$, i.e., 'slanderer'
($\delta\iota\alpha\beta\alpha\lambda\varepsilon\iota\nu$), heckle, speak ill of someone, calumniate).
So the calumniator and annihilator of a person's honour is the
very worst, the devil. Not only were men aware that such

slandering and dishonouring is diabolic; they also knew whence it came: from diabolical pride; oh yes, they always know – and never know! They also know well how much a man's honour is worth and what it means to destroy it; they know that the destroyer of a man's honour is a murderer of his personality, a murderer who brings civil death and civil hell upon his victim – for hell is part and parcel of the diabolical. Where Jews are concerned, however, they know nothing of this; where Jews are concerned, there can be no question of calumny or annihilating a person's honour; where Jews are concerned there is no such thing as honourable character, no conscience, no duty "to live and let live," no decency, no limit to what can be said and done against them.

Is this true? Do these things not exist in the case of Jews? And does it accord with conscience and decency for all these people to follow conscience and decency when they are in their own circle only but to cease to act thus when they move outside it? And it is true that human character can be split into two pieces like this, one piece beautiful and healthy and the other piece stinking and detestable? Can it be that, within the one human being, the *aristos*, the best person, the honourable person, lives side by side with the slanderer and the devil? Or is this impossible? Must we now regard character as unitary? What character is we can see in the case of the Jews. *Hic Rhodus, hic salta!*

5.

THE HATRED OF JEWS ACCELERATED THE DOWNFALL
OF GERMANY

And is it true that, in the case of Jews, no one knows
how loathsome *he* is who calls Jews loathsome? There is no
one anywhere who knows how loathsome he is and at what
point he has the power to be loathsome. And this not-knowing
is of prime importance. For what I am saying here (to my
reader from another planet, of course) is not meant as an
accusation against this society and against humanity. Any such
accusation would have neither success nor point. There are no
criminal investigations for the crimes of human society
committed down through history, least of all while mankind is
still committing these crimes; if it could sit in judgment on
itself on the Day of Judgment, there would still be no other
judge than mankind itself. And what is the point of merely
lamenting and complaining?

When basely treated, don't complain;

You'll yield to power just the same.

Baseness, which does not know that it is base, needs to be
ascertained and shown for what it is; so what we have said is
not an accusation against this society but – contrary to its
miserable babblings about its morality and its justice, contrary
to all the grand phrases that ought to make us blush with
shame – only a recognition of its nature, of human nature as a
whole, which takes every opportunity, always and at all points,
to show itself base; it is not just, for it misuses the words justice
and right.

Of course, this is an exaggeration, but again one sees and for the one who can see this is no exaggeration. We are only ascertaining the real nature of mankind, to which the Jews also belong; they are not better and more just simply because, in this period of history, they are the constant object of injustice and are powerless to act in a similarly unjust manner towards other human beings. All this is not an attack on men; they cannot be 'better' and different from what they are, for they too are thingly reality in motion within the general thingly reality in motion which is the world.

Anyone who is acquainted with the *Doctrine of Spiritual Élite and the Multitude* (see bibliography) and the theory of motion presented in it, will also understand human society as a motion in itself which cannot for a moment attain lasting being. Human beings live through one another and for one another in their society of honourable persons, but no one is prepared to punish and avenge. Those who take seriously the word 'Vengeance is mine' are not Christians; and those who know that they are in the One, and have unlearned the pride that sets them against their fellows, are not thinkers, not Spinozists. On the contrary, they hate one another out of pride and make each to sin against the other. So they are driven into conflict with one another, and everyone tries to drag the other down and get higher himself. In society's self-preservation the drive and the act of self-annihilation (self-annihilation in all relative existence) is always operative; they want to kill each other. The expressions of contempt, the insults, the calumnies are not, as yet, acts of murder, but they are on the way to becoming so, they are already murderous. They tend towards murder, to the diminishment of honour, to stripping others of honour, to civil liquidation; and from civil liquidation there is a strong impetus towards physical liquidation and total annihilation, which actually happens from time to time, on a small and a large scale.

Nothing is at rest within them; injustice is not at rest within them. This is simply a fact about human nature, not an accusation against man; human beings are unjust without wanting to be so and without being aware of it. They want to be just, because they regard being just as better than being unjust; they want to be the best and always think of themselves as the best, even with their wanton interest in injustice. Even what, in its innermost constitution, shows itself to be the ultimate egoistic injustice, does not seem so at all to them; to those who are totally incapable of consciousness of their own selves it appears to be morality, and the more they hide their own egoism, the more moral it seems. They can never consider themselves to be anything other than righteous, even in their most abominable and criminal acts. This is particularly so in the case of a group interest on the basis of pride, organized pride, for this gives the individuals a much finer conscience than, for instance, avarice. For avarice lends itself to solitary activity or only brings a few people together in league with one another; the dubious practices involved must be carried out secretly, and it is limited by the honour-interest, hence in most cases it still has conscience and a sense of shame. As for organized pride, however: 'They preen each other on promoting their evil cause and on their defamation of others. Their teaching is all pernicious lies; they will not be persuaded to do good but brood upon mischief in their lairs; they are firmly set upon an evil path and are not abashed at any wickedness' (Ps.96).   Organized pride glorifies the most heinous abuse. There is a commandment which says: 'Thou shalt not take the name of the Lord in vain', but none that says: 'Thou shalt not make abuse into a god.'   Organized pride enables all abominations to be freely performed in public; they can be carried out harmlessly, in simplicity of heart, in utter innocence of mind, faithfully and firmly, and those who do them seem to themselves and to the whole community to be inspired by the breath of the Holy Spirit.

Those who burnt heretics and witches were the most respected men in the society of their times, and all who assisted them were performing a work well-pleasing to God.   There is something in each individual which urges him to join in with the crowd and participate even in the most appalling abominations and crimes with red-hot enthusiasm and all the fanatical dramatics which belong to the hysteria of the crowd. Everyone joins in, everyone has it in him to do it to the others; it goes right to his heart, his heart swells with it; and no human being can be entirely purged of this poison.   This too, therefore, is not to denigrate the individual.   To denigrate the individual we would have to assert that individuals deliberately utter falsehood, slander others and treat them with malice. What we are saying, however, is that all this takes place unconsciously and that the most evil things appear to them, in their extraordinarily blinkered enthusiasms, to be good and best.   For we know how men deceive themselves about their own selves as a result of their moralistic criticism which masks their entire egoism.   Every egoist believes a liar.   He believes the moralist in him, the liar and self-deluder in him, who bestows the laurel of moralism on his egoism.   The only thing in nature that men know from within, themselves – O how they know themselves!   How little they know of their injustice and their pride.   The German still does not see that it was pride that brought him into his misfortune, and he is still pushing his pride further.

'May we not treat the Jews like this anymore? What, are we not supposed to be proud anymore? In that case, what would distinguish us from animals? Oh, we'll see about that. We are, and we remain, the best. No doubt these are lean times for pride, but we are not yet so unfortunate as to have to tolerate Jews among us. Where is our scapegoat, the Jew; where is he? Now you'll see how good we are, because our scapegoat, the Jew, is so bad. Quick, catch the scapegoat; look, he cannot defend himself as those outside can; here we have the power and the old, tried weapons of victory. Our virtue will triumph, we are the best. We always succeed in being the best against the defenceless.' That was the first thing Germany did, and in all truth it would have found much more to do and to mend. The Germans have sunk low. Far too many of them are in the grip of sloth, they have become dishonourable and corrupt, money-grabbing, cynical and completely twisted. So low can a nation be which has such pride – at the same time as it is so proud. For 'we sit down together so happily and are such good friends'.

Is this your philosophy, nation of philosophers? This is the question posed by your philosophy: Who is responsible for the War, the lost War, for all the misfortune that has happened and still threatens us, for revolution and Bolshevism? And this is the answer given by your philosophy: the Jews, the Jews are guilty; after them.

Nation of philosophers, with such elevated ideas you will not
attain a place in the history of philosophy, only in the history of
civilization; and there you stand already with your earlier
centuries, when you questioned so precisely and answered so
precisely when a blood sign stood in the heavens, or when a
war ended badly, or when there was famine or plague. You are
still the same nation of philosophers in the twentieth century.
Listen, O nation of philosophers, to one whom many consider
to be a philosopher; nothing that leads to evil and baseness is
genuine thought. For the second time you have taken your
watchword and your war-cry from those among you who are
basest and most stupid, from your Ahlwardts. O Germany, you
have wanted to establish your schools and universities on the
spirit, the hatred, of an Ahlwardt, to put worm-holes in your
most precious fruits. Is it possible that you can wallow in such
stupid hatred? You have forfeited, for a long time to come, a
historical influence. They have broken down your hedge,
destroyed your house, and you yourself are cursed by all the
world as the one who provoked this crisis for mankind; you are
hated by those who have power over you. But your pride is not
conquered. Each party still holds to its own egoism and its own
pride, absolutizing its own limitations, desecrating the
fatherland even further and rending it to shreds. And the
worst of all these rents is your hatred of Jews. Now
you have really and truly embraced hatred, blindly

hating out of pride. Now Germany's pride, in a radical and fanatical form, will make a path for itself where it can: with the evil, vengeful poison of humiliated pride, Germany will now hate wherever it still feels it has the upper hand; it makes such a noise with its hating that it does not hear that it itself is the object of hatred; and first and foremost the cry is: Get the Jews – for they cannot defend themselves: we are a hundred to one!

APPENDIX
Bolshevism And The Jews

After I had penned these lines I received a letter from a clergyman which prompted me to put together a full answer to the accusation concerning THE JEWS' AND BOLSHEVISM. I give it here as an appendix:

...I had not intended to write any more today, but I will and must write to you, the clergyman who once came to me for the sake of truth, through the *Doctrine of the Spiritual Élite and the Multitude.*

Today, again, you write: 'I wish at all costs to penetrate to the truth; and I sense that you are closest to it.' *In saying this you put me under an obligation* to reply to you concerning the second point of your letter (in spite of the fact that the first point seems so much more important today that I really wanted to limit myself to it alone). I sense, indeed I know, my dear Sir, from your observations on Bolshevism and the Jews' part in it, and by the fact that you think that it is at *the heart of the Jewish question*, that you are by no means close to the truth but to confusion and error.

Even without being an anti-Semite, you should not entertain these views nor have any contact with confusion and error. For it is confusion to look for the heart of the Jewish question, and the excuse for the antisemitism which causes you such painful regret (the antisemitism of those whom, with you I call the "multitude") in the part the Jews have played in Bolshevism and in the tendency of the Jewish leaders of the radical parties of the left to 'push themselves forward.' How long will you go on confusing some Jews with all Jews, to confuse individual Jews with others who are diametrically opposed to them and seek to work against them? Men can be Bolshevists, and others can be capitalists and Mammonists, without it being necessary to say that all men are Bolshevists or all are capitalists and Mammonists and that the heart of the human question lies in Bolshevism or capitalism and Mammonism.

So now the heart of the Jewish question is supposed to have been found, most recently, by sleight of hand, in Bolshevism; for am I not right in thinking that yesterday most people thought they had found it in Mammonism – and largely still do? Or are capitalism and Bolshevism the same thing, both belonging to the Jew? As the Coptic Christians, for instance, practised both baptism *and* circumcision? Indeed, it is as if they wanted to show how they used their stupidities to pass the intelligence test, when we read today, in antisemitic publications, that capitalism *and* Bolshevism are the Jews' cunning means of attaining power, i.e., that capitalism and Bolshevism form the twin kernels of the Jewish question – whereas the kernel of the Jewish question is the question of antisemitism, and the kernel of antisemitism is pride, memsheleth sadon! What might *not* be the kernel of the Jewish question, if we were to look for it and determine to find it wherever Jews are deeply involved and exercise leadership? – and there is no need to speak of them 'pushing themselves forward'. Jews play their part in all the parties (except, naturally, in those where hatred of Jews keeps them away), because these parties are not slow to use the Jews' abilities. How could they ever take a leading role anywhere unless they were put into it by the majority, the non-Jews, who have confidence in their abilities and character? If they were simply pushing themselves forward they would soon find themselves pushed back again. No. Where Jews are at the helm of a party, and the party eventually becomes a governing party, be it sooner or later, Jews will be at the helm of government; precisely because they were formerly at the helm of the party. In any case, it is not so easy to push oneself forward. If you think – for whatever reasons or non-reasons – that it *is* easy in the case of the Liberals, Democrats, Socialists, Independents, Communists and Bolshevists – there are still the Conservatives, who will certainly not make it easy for a Jew to push his way to the top as their leader. Did the Jew, Friedrich Julius Stahl [1802-1861], become the founder and first leader of the Conservative Party simply by pushing himself forward? And should we see the kernel of the Jewish question, then, in the fact (among others things) that the Jew, Stahl, formulated the programme of the Conservative Party? My dear Sir, are human beings, in all their diversity, going to make the Jews out to be monsters to a man, to make them into the devil, to whom only damned souls would ever light a candle, simply on account of all these diverse possibilities and realities of the human spirit?[2]

---

[2] I have just received a small volume entitled 'Deutscher Geist und Judenhass. Ausserungen nicht jüdischer Zeitgenossen' (Kulturverlag, Berlin 1920), which incidentally contains gratifying statements from a considerable number of your colleagues. In this collection I find the following observations by Professor Quidde of Munich regarding the 'forward' and 'obtrusive' nature of Jews: 'If a party in a particular constituency has 10,000 electors, of whom 1,000 are Jews (i.e., 10%), and if they are organized into an association of 1,000 members, there will be far more than 100 Jews among these 1,000, possibly 300 (i.e., 30%). If this association calls a meeting of members, at which 100 members attend, you can be sure that far more than 30 of them will be Jews, more like 60 (i.e., 60%). And when debating begins, how many of the speakers will be Jews? People complain that the Jews push themselves forward. Rather, they should complain of the inertia of the non-Jews.

Here is another example. Years ago, in Reichenhall, I met Dr. Langerhans, who had been Chairman of the Berlin City Council for a long time. He said how difficult it was to avoid an undesirably high prominence of Jews in the City Council. When looking for someone to present a paper, for instance, he would initially approach the most competent person, a Jew. The latter would say he was willing, but would ask to be left out on this occasion, lest people should say, "a Jew again!" Then he would approach three, four or five Christians, one after another, but each one would refuse; one would say

Don't talk to me about the Jews being the sinners responsible for the misfortune of Bolshevism! And although both of us are convinced that Bolshevism signifies our civilization's great misfortune – and it would assuredly bring misfortune upon all of us – what good is this conviction? Let me remind you of what I have said on this subject, and how convictions are formed: they are based on nothing but interests.

---

he did not feel up to the task, another would not take on the work involved, the third had far too much to do, the fourth had some domestic celebrations to attend to, etc. Finally he was obliged to approach the Jewish member again, and so there would be talk of "Jews once more pushing themselves forward." Many of those involved in the parties pursuing freedom and in all circles of cultural progress will be obliged to confirm that, when it is a question of a greater readiness for sacrifice, not only in terms of money but also in terms of work-load, not only where a high profile is required but also where there is hidden work to be done, and even when external honours are not to be gained, it is Jewish colleagues, again and again, who can be relied on. The reason why Jewry plays a particularly prominent role in public life today is simply that, in earlier years, almost all the non-Jewish intellectuals neglected to involve themselves with the socialist workers' movement. Judaism has provided the Social Democratic movement with its indispensable spiritual leaders. The Revolution has thus brought the Jewish element to the top along with socialism.   It is the non-Jews who are inclined towards socialism who are at fault; they lacked the courage, earlier, to show their colours. Non-Jews should simply match Jews in their active efforts towards the common good and their involvement in it. This would soon cut down to size the in many ways disproportionate Jewish influence. But instead of making such efforts, it is much more convenient to repeat slogans such as, "All misfortune comes from the Jews, so let's kill the Jews!" Baseness, sloth and the lack of ability join hand in hand. Then the whole thing is covered with a threadbare cloak of patriotism. That is antisemitism.'

(And here, of course, I am only speaking of convictions which pass over into practice, not of intellectual concepts and our reflections upon what is eternal.) If *you* had lived in the Roman Empire at the time Judaism was arising, you would most probably have shared the conviction of the entire world then, that those Jews were pernicious and execrable, with their nonsense about renewing the world, no more afraid of dying for their nonsensical convictions than our Bolshevists are, including the Jews among them–for it is a fact that many leading Bolshevists are Jews. In the event, the whole world allowed itself to be convinced of the rightness of that Judaism alias Christianity, and even today *you*, for instance, are a Christian priest, that is, a priest of that Judaism.

I am the last person to want to put Bolshevism on the same level with Christianity or Judaism. I am only speaking of the relativity of our convictions and the injustice of condemning others because of their convictions. Conviction is conviction in everyone who is convinced; the Bolshevist is no less convinced–simply as regards conviction itself–than you or I. And it is certainly unjust in the extreme to hold Jewry, the Jews as a body, responsible for Bolshevism, and to want to see in that the kernel of the Jewish question. Don't become one of those nut-crackers looking for the kernel of the Jewish question–for there is no Jewish question: there is only a...question! The question is, will *you* open your eyes and see what is there, namely, that Jews–as if they were human beings like other human beings – are capable of all the diverse things that human beings are capable of. You need to open your eyes and see that men's thoughts are as varied as their interests, and you must not close your eyes when it comes to Jews. The Jews must finally be allowed to be human beings; they must be allowed to have equal rights as factotum, not merely as facbonum: they must have equal rights to engage in all the same nonsense and immaturity as other people, and under certain circumstances they must be allowed even to be as intelligent, useful and admirable as the person who is giving his verdict about them. Nor should it be said that they *must* be mad and dangerous because other Jews in other parties are mad and dangerous. We should not be continually speaking of 'the Jews' when what we mean is that particular kind of Jew whose convictions are repugnant to other Jews no less than to us. Do you really want to use the Jews as a cloth to mop up your anger over Bolshevism? What about the Jews who are Liberals, Democrats, Social Democrats, Independent Social Democrats? What about the Zionist Jews? Do you know that at the present time ninety per cent of all Jews are Zionists? If you take away from the remaining ten per cent the Jews who are Liberals, Democrats, Social Democrats, and Independent Social Democrats, do you still really want to hold all Jewry responsible for Bolshevism? In the 'Central Association of German Citizens of Jewish Faith' there are perhaps 200,000 or 300,000 Jews who profess German nationality and *Jewish faith*; you can be quite sure that not a single one of them can be

called a Bolshevist. Do you want to go on? Your God was
prepared to spare Sodom and Gomorrah for the sake of ten
righteous men, and you are prepared to make all Jewry into a
Bolshevist Sodom and Gomorrah for the sake of a few Jews
who are involved in Bolshevism! You should not continue to
speak like this about the Jews. Speaking about Jews like this
testifies to a disgraceful sloth and flippancy in judgment, and
leads to malicious injustice and base deeds, if not in ourselves,
then in others on our account. Someone might not need to be
ashamed of his own actions, but he would still have cause to be
ashamed of more than simply his judgment. We must turn our
backs both on base deeds and the world's nonsensical
judgment; we must not join in them; for we actually strengthen
the world's base practice if we show ourselves weak against its
judgment and prejudice. We must turn aside from its paths
and walk the royal road of thought. My dear Sir, you yourself
must use your mind in these matters too..., *nor must you
continually succumb to what your newspapers and your
acquaintances say.* What do you mean, in your letter, by once
more praising 'the lofty citadel' of my book on the Jews?
Surely you do not mean that, even for a single train of thought,
you are prepared to occupy a low citadel?

I am putting this thus plainly to you, otherwise our
relationship and friendship would be meaningless, an
absurdity. Just this once, I ask you to contemplate the matter
in hand *not* from the heights of the citadel – which in any case

you no longer use in your contemplations. It is difficult, true; almost more difficult than separating oneself, in a theoretical and philosophical way, from men's usual ideas and affirming that these ideas have no claim to truth outside the day-to-day practical concerns of the human being; which is equivalent to separating oneself from human beings to some extent. But we must separate ourselves from men to that extent if we are daily to become surer of authentic truth, and of life according to truth in life's eternal fullness, and if we are to be able to dedicate ourselves to men in the best possible manner and surrender to them the best that we have. It is unimaginably hard, when engaged in the details of contemplation and action, not to become contaminated again and again by our environment – as you have been in the case before us. I beg you to read again and attend to the passage in my *Deutschenhass, Judenhass und Judenhass der Deutschen*, pp. 58-60 (as I think you only have the first edition of my *Judenbuch*):

'We must demand that the political parties separate themselves from the anti-Semites. So far the parties have not really done this. In fact (and this obliges us to be even sharper in our criticism of them) they have joined forces with the anti-Semites more closely than ever now, at a time when the flames of hatred of Jews are once more burning high. And this is understandable, for once again, on a scale hitherto hardly known, people are being stirred up to join in a man-hunt. They are always easily led in this direction. This time, however, they are being incited to hunt down the Jews, since the Jews are responsible for Communism. But why should the Jews not be responsible for Communism? Why exclude Communism? After all, the Jews are responsible for everything, and that includes Communism. As we know, the Jews are also responsible for Social Democracy, the Jews are also responsible for Liberalism, and the Jews are also responsible for the Conservative Party. For the latter still stands on the basis laid down by the Jew, Stahl. Why should Jews not try to introduce Communism and become leading Communists, since they have already been able to become leading Social Democrats, leading Liberals, leading Conservatives, as well as being the founders of these parties. Jews, evidently, can become everything: anti-Semites can become nothing; they can only be anti-Semites. They can become nothing, even against Jews, even if they go as far as pogroms – probably because Jews, in their turn, can become everything, except anti-Semites. Indeed, in general terms, what have the Jews not created? Not only Judaism, but Christianity as well. Jews can do everything, and anti-Semites can do nothing: that's that. How ridiculous it all is. Jews are not as obviously and one-sidedly 'the Jews' as anti-Semites are 'the anti-Semites'; Jews do not occupy such a specialist role in the world at all. Jews are human beings and, like other human beings, they can be, become and do all manner of things. Jews are and remain human beings in our world; no antisemitism can change that.

So how ridiculous it is, in general, to be an anti-Semite because of the Communism of certain Jews, after having been so earnestly and so long an anti-Semite because of the capitalism of other Jews. As for the Jews and Communism, surely this ought to diminish hatred of Jews rather than increase it?

In no country would antisemitism be as ridiculous as in Germany; nor as suicidal: if Germany can bring no more evidence for damning the Jews than it has produced so far, it must stop damning them, or else it will keep on damning itself along with them.

What more can be said to Germany, in future, than this one thing? What other answer can be given if it continues to solve 'the Jewish question' by engaging in a campaign of slander? – 'The Jewish question': what a stupid expression. The fact that there are Jews is no more a 'question' than that there are anti-Semites; and in any case the Jewish question only exists for those who have the antisemitic answer. And the more Jewish question and antisemitic answer there is in Germany, the sooner we will be able to silence all other words and weapons and, finally, say just this: first you get rid of the hatred of Germans from the world so that we can distinguish your hatred of Jews, your hating, from your being hated; then, when you Germans have less hatred, slandering and pride among yourselves, between your parties, your hatred and slandering of Jews and your arrogance towards them will really be something distinctive of you!'

All this brings pain and a sense of disgrace to every thinking German in whom there burns a feeling for the unity of the fatherland, because he has grasped the idea of the fatherland in its depth and breadth and loves his fatherland and his people – pain and disgrace, to think that the entire Conservative Party has sunk so low. I keep talking about the Conservatives, for the Conservatives must and will remain the Conservatives; they must not be absorbed into this German nationalism, and eventually, compelled by necessity, they will break off their present connection (and one day, perhaps, all connection whatsoever) with the anti-Semites. In the words of Oppeln-Bronikowski: the Conservatives must turn aside from the 'madness of antisemitism'; they must climb down and stop putting all their courage into pride; they must see to it that their patriotism does not turn straight away into insolence and sick rage; they must no longer take prescriptions from Doctor Ahlwardt ('Get the Jews – they cannot defend themselves!'). Thus the Conservatives have set upon the wretched fatherland which has lost this War and still does not know what it means to have lost this War; it seems to believe only that it hasn't lost enough yet, and it seems to think only about how it can pursue the war of annihilation against itself to the bitter end. A nation that smashes itself to pieces – how can such a nation rise again in the world?

One must, absolutely must, get out of this situation in which the country is torn asunder by parties. But how can there be understanding and agreement without the requisite good will? How can this come about where the only reasons adduced are party reasons, which arise simply from egoism in each case, and where there is no good will but only ill will and our sick mutual relationships? And in commending good will, I do not mean the good will manifested in the fondness of love but the good will of sound health and reason which does not, in myopic party blindness, destroy both the nation and its own party.

For the Germans are a mixture, a cross of the most various races, made up of pre-Germanic and pre-Indo-European original inhabitants, Germanic tribes, Wends, Poles, Lithuanians, Cassubians, Celts, Jews; it forms the German conglomerate within the great white race. So I still say, with Friedrich Müller: 'Racial theories are pure humbug!' No one would take any notice of it if it did not moisten the throats of the Jew-haters and haters of human beings, enabling them to crow their watchword, "Get the Jews – the Jews cannot defend themselves!" (End of the letter to the clergyman.)

6.

LOVE OF THE ONE *VERSUS REASONING ARISING FROM INTEREST*

The Jews cannot defend themselves, and yet they must defend themselves, for good or ill. They must fight. Things have improved to the extent that today they can at least fight, whereas yesterday and for almost two millennia they were a completely passive historical quantity, subject to anything and everything. The emancipation of Jews has begun. It has only just begun; it is a slow historical process, but one of incalculable significance; for it transforms the Jews once more into a force that is active in history. It liberates the energies of these human beings, who are not only useful to society but also important for human history; it liberates the Jews with their great ethos. Will they succeed in the role of a lover (of mankind) they have played so far, and will human history really come to a virtuous conclusion, as the Jews' prophets (with the exception of their greatest prophet) have promised? I do not think so; in any case it would take a very long time to reach the future to which this conclusion refers; and the conclusion itself, the future state of happiness and justice, could easily be very short. Oh dear, we cannot even say that the future is short, for the future is never; and what use to mankind is the justice that limps behind it! At all events it seems certain that the Jews will continue to play their part and be necessary to the world. There will be no exchanging of roles with the anti-Semites. If they were called upon to show their paces, if they were to get into the fatal situation of having to manifest gifts and a soul – they are by nature simply not called to it. The anti-Semites could never produce Judaism, or what is exactly the same, Christianity, i.e., the Bible and the continuation of the Bible, everything that seeks to implement the spirit of the Bible. Social Democracy is part and parcel of this, and the 'Doctrine of the Spiritual Élite and the Multitude,' the possible completion of Christianity where it can be completed, and since here human nature does not stand in the way, as in the case of the generality of men. (For this was the great misunderstanding, to imagine that it could be implemented among the generality of men. And as sure as I was brought forth from the dark womb into the light of day, so this teaching will be brought into life and implemented, through my life, albeit after my death.) The anti-Semites produce wretched things lacking all spirit; they do not possess the gifts and the ethos of Jews. Their pride, which lashes out in all directions, and their hostility to Jews are even less able to compensate for this lack, since history is evidently interested, not in mere equality of rights for Jews but actually in their non-equality; an antisemitic wind swells the Jewish sails. After the historical role played by Jews hitherto it seems that far more is at stake than the struggle between anti-Semites and Jews and all that comes into consciousness as a result. Far more is at stake than the pride of the anti-Semites and the sufferings of the Jews.

The emancipation of the Jews does not need to signify that the Jews are emancipated and really have equal rights, having attained to personal dignity and honour.   History has no interest in such things; history too is only concerned with its own interest; the concept of suffering means nothing to it. For history, the Jews (with their suffering) are only a medium for Judaism, and in turn the anti-Semites (with their pride) simply act as catalysts in the production of this medium.

There can be no doubt that the anti-Semites contribute substantially to the Jews' Jewishness; in fact, they keep alive the very thing they imagine they are combating. Without antisemitism the Jews would gradually become assimilated to non-Jews and amalgamate with them, and Judaism would disappear.   Without anti-Semites and unmerited suffering, therefore, there would soon be no Jews at all (just as rich men die of an easy life, but not of anxieties concerned with business). So the question is not, what are the rights of Jews, but this: are the Jews to get their rights and thus perish, or are they to continue to exist in injustice? *Aut pati, aut mori*; they must either suffer or die. So too there can be no remedy for the Jews against antisemitism, for antisemitism itself is actually a factor that encourages Jews. Thus, shrewdly and simply, history uses this ever-present domestic prescription of antisemitism – with its donkey's ears (see p. 40 above) and its total lack of spirit – to stimulate the spirit of Judaism. History is concerned with Judaism, and hence with Jews and hence too with anti-Semites, whose task is to perform the miracle of eternalizing Jewish blood – most definitely one of the greatest miracles to happen to the Jews. What was the Jews' crossing of the Red Sea in ancient times, compared with this eternal crossing of the Red Sea by Jews?!

History is concerned with Judaism, and it should be more important for us, too, to get to know the essence of Judaism than the essence and grotesque nature of antisemitism. With regard to the essence of Judaism, then, the Jews ought surely to know more; ordinarily they are unwilling, and know nothing of their heritage but the guilt attributed to them, the hardships and calamities associated with it. It would be good for Jews to know something of Judaism; then they could make their houses warm – as one keeps a fire in winter time – and would be better able to endure the harsh life outside. For it is highly doubtful that their lot in the outside world will soon change in the way they would wish. There is an improvement already once they feel that it is not so great a misfortune; that in itself changes their lot, even if it stays the same. In any case it would be greatly to be wished that they would be clear about their task and situation; for clarity is the beginning of all improvement, and to be familiar with a danger means that one is far less threatened by it, and correspondingly happier. One could wish that they were proud of their cultural importance – proud, but not arrogant. Arrogance is an unjustified sense of self that expresses itself in contempt of others, whereas a proper pride is a genuine, justified sense of self that is in touch with one's own being; it provides protection against the arrogance of others. Due pride versus arrogance! Every Jew could be proud, for it is the spirit of his community, surging round him from all points; his pride could be sweeter to him than all honours, and he would need to be unaffected by the arrogance of this society, to which he can say: 'What is best in you has come from us!' Jews could be all the more proud, the more they are exposed to the arrogance of the others and the less recognition they receive – as if history had given them the privilege of achieving great things in a purely objective way, without being honoured for them.

Yes, it seems that history has appointed Jews to be the target of injustice; by definition they seem to be human beings who, for some profound reason, are denied the satisfaction of honour and of vanity. But, since they are not also denied the longing for these things, the Jews' situation is bad enough. Individual Jews are thoroughly ordinary men, they are not 'a nation of priests', a 'holy people', they are not Christians or Jews of the prophetic tradition, and they *do not think* – they are ordinary human beings. And to ask Jews to put up with it: 'We have been appointed to suffer injustice' – is to expect ordinary men to be extraordinary men. It is to expect them to have within them, not the ordinary consciousness, but the historical and spiritual consciousness; it is to expect them not to be afraid of arrogance, of men and of the world because they have perceived the insubstantiality of the world and know that they are more than 'world'. In other words it is to expect Jews to endure disregard and disdain with the consciousness and strength of geniuses. What does it mean to ordinary people to make demands to them which would require them to be more than ordinary people? To them – who regard ordinary men as men pure and simple, and could not possibly envisage there being any other kind of human being, spiritual human beings, in whom everything is different – it suggests, to human beings in their weakness and ordinariness, that they are less than human beings; it signifies their extinction of the self.

Ordinary, weak men fear the world's pride, because they themselves are world, nothing but world. Jews could easily be arrogant and deprive others of their honour-vanity, and in their own eyes they would seem justified in doing so. But if others who are arrogant come and take away *their* honour-vanity, they are bound to feel that they have been made less than human beings and that this is an injustice, since they lack the compensation of historically important achievements and the creative energy found in genius. The achievements of genius, in so far as they come from Jews, are only produced by the geniuses among them. And geniuses have been endowed by nature with the ability to be sufficient unto themselves in a bitter-tasting destiny, to accept suffering and being misunderstood; in the depths of their souls they are enabled to disavow, as it were, even the most appalling things that happen to them, as if they dreamed them; as if this life, both existing and no longer existing, were part of a dream. Granted that perhaps the most genial things the world has to show, and certainly the most influential things in it, have emerged from the Jewish community, and that it may have equally important things to produce in the future: it would be a mistake to condemn all individual Jews to the fate of the genius and expect them to accept suffering and being misunderstood, to accept being slaves under tyrants (Isa 49:7), 'an astonishment, a proverb, and byword among all nations whither the Lord shall lead them' (Deut 28:37). The Lord, or history itself, can deal thus with the Jews on the basis of higher reasons and superior power, but to expect all these Jews to even understand this, let alone be content with it...? All these lives want to live, not in history, but in life; the whole of world history and the universe is not worth as much to them as their own life; and as for the spirit of Judaism, as we have said, it only lives in those among the Jews who are geniuses; it is not the sum total of Jews, nor some multiple of them. What distinguishes the great from the small and petty is that the great, the geniuses, actually *will* what they ought to do and must do. Thus Socrates *wills* to drink the poison cup, Christ *wills* to take up his cross; and how Spinoza accepted his ignominy and used it! But the Jews, all the ordinary Jews, are incapable of willing what they ought to do and must do. Human beings that they are, whose consciousness tells them that they exist for their own sake, claiming to have a right to live among other human beings and being incapable of ridding their consciousness of the concept of honour, the Jews must say No to the unequalled cruelty with which their fullness of life, the fullness of their entire world, has been violated. They must resist all the hangmen who come to execute judgment upon them. No; they are unwilling to be the chosen target for the world's injustice and to be regarded as swindlers. In earlier times many a person played the part of a fool in order to stay alive, but no one can adopt the role of the crook and even less can the Jews *be* swindlers simply because the anti-Semites call them such. No; Jews are not willing to be exposed to contempt, hatred and persecution for no other reason than that they are called Jews; they are not prepared to accept that society, whenever it feels particularly miserable or particularly elated, should unleash its canaille on them.

But even if they are unwilling and say No, history wills it thus; so the Jews' No is a powerless No: they must suffer their destiny. History does not ask the Jews first; each of them has a good mother, but in history he has a harsh mother. History no more asks the Jews than it asks the anti-Semites, who would doubtless not be inclined to be grateful for the Jews' significance and for all Jews. This is the ultimate point: if the Jews are an organ of history, and to the extent that they are such, their individual consciousness is of no account. They remain unaware of the depth and breadth of the 'whence' and 'whither' of their primary significance. All they have is the individual consciousness of the motives which maintain them in life; they do not possess the great ONE, they possess neither the One of the world nor the ONE of eternity, but only the little 'one' of their 'I's and their aura of mist, the clouds which conceal from them their higher light. They may perceive and speak, or be dumb; they may fail to perceive, ruining their spirit by the way they live their lives and conduct themselves; they may wage war on their historical mission and truth, trying to upset it and suffering as result, for they are bound to serve it all the same. If only they would serve it. Whether they will or not, and however much suffering it involves. For why should not a community, too, bear what the genius has to bear? The individual has relatively little strength to bear it, but the strength of the whole suffices. History does not want to know whether it harms those who serve it; history has no feelings for what the latter may suffer.

Nor had we, basically, in the matter which interests and concerns us here. It was not our intention to annihilate antisemitism, for instance, but only to perceive and characterize it, only to think about it. Hopefully we have achieved this to some extent, and our readers have not found it difficult. Usually people say, 'Thinking, Oh dear! Why make life difficult for oneself?!' – not realizing how difficult they make life by not thinking. Nothing makes life as difficult as non-thinking. How simple thinking is, and if everyone were to think, how simple life would be!

Thinking makes things easier, even in the society of non-thinkers; how splendid life must be, therefore, in a society of thinkers!   But unfortunately this is only something for the imagination.   (Naturally I am only speaking of real thinking – philosophy, which heals headaches, not scholasticism, which creates them.)   Thinking is so easy; one only needs to lose one's reason a little.   For with the practical reason it is impossible to think or understand anything. Practical reason, i.e., ordinary feeling, knowing and willing, is only useful for living, as people ordinarily live.   If one only has the interests, and imaginary and improper interests, of love, possession and prestige, of honour-vanity and arrogance, then, whether one's methods are right or wrong, one is only pursuing one's own egoism.   That is the way life's practical reason operates; and if we are to be able to think, we must lose some of it.   For in using this reason we have not got as far as thinking; it only gives us consciousness of, and the means to provide for, life and our humannes, our animal nature, our thingly nature, our worldly nature.   This does not mean that we should 'not care about anything that is of the world'; but we should only refrain from making the world absolute.   Nor does it mean that we must lose the interest of love, of possession and of prestige – for that would mean losing life itself.   But what we should lose is the imaginary and improper, the unrestrained and exclusive interest which causes us to think of nothing beyond our interests and supposed interests, swilling injustice like water; it is this that prevents us from placing ourselves, outside our own interest, before the reality of the facts.

For this is what thinking is. There is nothing more profound to it. This is the whole of thinking in its life-size proportions. Recipe: simply put yourself in front of reality; thus you will enter the forest of thought, be launched on the ocean of thought, into freedom and greatness. Put yourself in the presence of reality; that way you will be able to survive the onslaught of interests and to identify the interest-related judgments and prejudices (which are the same thing) as error, contrary to the truth, and give them up since they are irreconcilable with the facts. That is thinking. And anyone who wants to think about the Jews must also think in this way; first of all he must extract himself from interest, i.e., antisemitism; and if he cannot, let him not imagine that he is in a position to think about the Jews. For antisemitism is an interest-related judgment that comes from self-seeking. All judgments come from self-seeking, from interest-related thought, and have nothing to do with the real interest of thinking. Only where the interest of thinking is alive does the truth of thinking come, not from self-seeking, but from the love of the ONE; or rather, the knowledge of the truth (really standing in and before reality, both exterior and interior reality) is the same as the love of the ONE. This love is entirely different from the love which comes from self-seeking in our relative consciousness. You, with all your judgments and ideas: do not trust your judgments and ideas, but look, keep on looking! And if others are worse than you, it is high time for you to take a look and see whether you are not worse than they. O wretched man you are if you are arrogant! For that means that you have entered into the narrowness and wretchedness of your thingly nature (which is *not yours*): i.e., you have lost what is genuinely yours, namely, the connection with the Whole and the ONE, with the eternity and blessedness of knowledge and love. You have become an unthinking thing in the vast breadth of things, a stupid, transitory speck of filth in clouds of darkness and fog, imagining itself to be great because it stinks more than other filth. But man, how sublime you are once you actually think! Then, in the depth of yourSelf, you are light and the eternal ONE, knowledge of genuine reality, love; then you know the world and its injustice without being entangled in it; you are world and yet free of the world and blessed, you are the I, the All and the ONE.

They do not think, i.e., they do not see what is real. They see only their interests and supposed interests, and their minds are concerned with nothing but these interests. They love what is least significant, and what they call 'love' is demanded by the interest of their extremely narrow self-love, the male and female forms of self-love, and the self-love expressed in proofs of friendship. (Christ did not want to have anything to do with what men call 'love', and spoke of the self-seeking involved in it: anyone who did not love him more than father, mother, wife and child, was not worthy of him, i.e., did not really love.) And men have so much contempt, and hate, hate and hate! Their loving unites them with very few others and it is an interest of no higher value than their possession-interest or honour-interest, which separates them from many of their fellows. They do not love intrinsically, consequently they are not happy, not blissful; and between *their* little loving and their much contempt and hating there is the vast area of 'What's that to me?' And their contempt and hatred comes mainly from arrogance. That is their non-thinking, by which they make life hard and dreadful for one another. Why do people not see this? Just take one look and see that most human unhappiness comes from this hatred! Just think – and there is no need, afterwards, to go on thinking about this and apply it, if you cannot – but just this moment, reading these lines, while there is no other interest interfering with your thinking of it, just this once have pity on your soul and your thinking, and do not consider yourself either too high or to low to think about this: how much hating goes on in our world without the person hated giving any cause for it. In only very few cases is such hatred, passionate hatred, justified, inevitable and understandable, as it were – people being as they are – as an impotent resistance to continually inflicted injustice, viz. against oppression. Against such action there can be no other equivalent reaction but hatred.

But all this hatred which arises out of, and together with, pride and its injustice?   Our understanding of hatred remains incomplete unless we give prime attention to this chief hate, which is not the passionate reaction of the person who continually suffers injustice, of the oppressed, but the hate which comes from 'the right hand and the left hand indiscriminately', the hate arising from the perpetration of some misdeed, together with imaginary wickedness attributed to the person hated and the anticipated reaction to his wickedness. This hate does not come from powerlessness, but from the power of the hater and *from pride frustrated in its goal*. Nor should we immediately ask what the person hated has done to the one who hates. An equally good question is: What has the hater done to the object of his hate? The cause of a person's being hated seldom lies in him; usually it lies in the one who hates him. If only people could think of *that*! Indeed, if they could only *think*! The reasons for hating lie deep in human nature, in man's non-thinking nature.   Anyone who grasps the fact that human beings cannot think, or (which comes to the same thing) who grasps the teaching of Judaism and Christ on the sinfulness of all men, which accords with the teaching of the Stoics, such a person understands the basis of hate.

Such a person also understands antisemitism and what we have said about the Jews being not the cause but only the catalyst of hatred. It is totally inadequate to say that the fault must lie with the Jews if the whole world is so against them.

The whole world is similarly against the whole world, in so far as it can. The question of pride and hatred is not exclusive to the 'Jewish question.' What in our case is called hatred of Jews has different names in different places; it is found throughout the whole of mankind as hatred of the human being. Who is prepared to understand this and take pains to unlearn the most hideous of all practices, to which the hatred of Jews belongs? Once the hatred of Jews is understood to be hatred of the human being, simply called 'hatred of Jews' in our case, bearing a different name elsewhere, and to be found everywhere (this is shown in more detail in *Der Judenhass und die Juden*), this hatred of Jews loses all meaning; then it becomes impossible to say that the Jews are at fault because of this and that. Who is prepared to understand that hatred of Jews tells us nothing about Jews but a great deal about all the world? The whole world is against the whole world, in so far as it can be, and the extremity of this hostility is seen in its attitude towards the Jews. It is not the Jews who are at fault: what is responsible is the interest against them, i.e., pride and the hating nature of those who hate them. *The hater is responsible, not the hated*, otherwise all human beings would have to be scoundrels, which in fact they are not, except in the judgment of their haters. There is not a single human being, however noble and sublime, of whom someone who feels an interest against him has not said: '*I* know him – the scoundrel!' But his friends, who have a different and better knowledge of him than his enemies, speak well of him rather than evil.[3]

---

[3] This seems to be different, however, in the case of the most sublime human beings, the leaders of the anti-Semites. None of these anti-Semites thinks as badly of Jews as he does of anti-Semites; and since it is their aim to heap the most vicious insults and calumnies on each other, it is naturally not enough for them to call each other anti-Semites: they must make each other out to be Jews. See the illuminating and delightful remarks on this subject in *Der Judenhass und die Juden*, p. 86ff. See also p. 236ff, which gives an account of the vast numbers of men whom antisemitic research has found to be Jews, including – for science is implacable in its workings – the most respected men of our world, e.g., Rembrandt, Lessing, Goethe, Hebbel, Nietzsche, Bismarck; indeed, if it were to go on like this, there would be no non-Jews left of any consequence. Yes; science is implacable and *does* go on: the great numbers of men found to be Jews are growing at such a rate – and here I hope to crown my efforts on behalf of antisemitism by making the following suggestion. In order to achieve the widest possible circulation of the antisemitic discoveries, instead of printing fat books (as at present) containing the names of the unmasked Jews, books that can only be produced at the cost of much money and tedium, one should simply print quite slender volumes containing the few names and addresses of those who are not Jews. For now sometimes even a single Jew, shamelessly, takes up a whole book: only recently it took a book entitled *Semi-Imperator 1888-1918*, 206 pages strong (or weak), to show that one of the worst Jews, Wilhelm II, was a Jew. Wilhelm II is once more 'compelling proof that blood, not education, is the determining factor.' It is this Jew who brought Germany into the abyss. It is shown from his mental characteristics that he was a Jew: the Jews are known to have a histrionic talent, and so did Wilhelm II. 'It was all *acting*: he played the monarch by God's grace who had succumbed to the illusion of being a Caesar, the victorious general, the art and music critic, the painter, preacher, composer; he acted the part of the Christian ruler, held religious services and spoke a great deal about the Christian state....The Jewish wanderlust in him made him into a traveling Emperor.' But his Jewish descent is also shown in physiological and genealogical terms and illustrated by means of pictures of him.

122

And so it is with Jews and their enemies, for the latter believe
that it simply cannot be otherwise: they would be bound to

What is not proclaimed and named and 'nosed' to be Jewish! But
recently even the Jews themselves have started this absurd kind of research
and are making anti-Semites into Jews. In my view they should be content
with the antisemitic Jews who are notorious Jews and not set their hearts on
more birds of this kind. For instance, they should leave Adolf Bartels alone;
all the same, in spite of his name, he.... Certainly, the name Bartels is Jewish,
one half of the Jewish name Bartollmai, Bartholomew, which gives us two
names, Bartels and Mewes (or Möbius). Bartels is the first half of the
Hebrew name Bartollmai with the addition of an 's', i.e., it is really Bartolls.
Bartollmai means 'son of Tollmai'; the name Tollmai occurs in Joshua 15:14
and 2 Sam 13:37. Bar means 'son' and Tollmai means Tollmai, i.e., it is a
proper name; the 's' at the end of a proper name also means 'son' (i.e.,
Jacobs, Stephens, Mertens are the same as Jacobssohn, Sephenssohn,
Mertenssohn – such names are called patronymics, that is, 'called after the
father'). Literally, therefore, Bartels means 'son of Toll's son'; for Bartels is
originally Bartolls, and Bar means 'son' and toll means toll (as part of a
proper name), and 's' again means 'son'. But does this prove that Bartels is a
Jew? Jews should not adopt from anti-Semites the practice of drawing
conclusions from names; they should leave poor Bartels in peace, they should
refrain from flaying this Bartholomew alive; otherwise he will end up
considering himself a Jew after all, like the Bartholomew who was flayed, and
a saint and an apostle. I do not know, either, whether he is a Jew or not, nor
what kind of nose he has; I cannot even tell whether he has a Jewish or Aryan
spirit, since I have never even seen a line of his – not even what he wrote in
praise of my German name. Naturally, for reasons of egoism, this influences
me (even without having read it) to come to his defence on account of his
Hebrew name and assert that, in spite of this Hebrew name, as I have said, it
does not mean that Bartels is really a Jew or even merely exhibits Jewish
spirit. No more, naturally, than he exhibits Aryan spirit. Since he is an anti-
Semite, I assume that he has no spirit whatsoever, which he himself is
supposed to have shown convincingly in his writings. Even anti-Semites
urged me, rather than reading something by Bartels, to write something
about myself, since *Bartels's only value was as an anti-Semite*. Heavens!
That's how it goes: I did not want to write anything bad about the man, and
now there it is! Incidentally it seems to me that the fact that Bartels really
exhibits no spirit is indicated and prophesied, with magnificent profundity, by
his strange double patronymic: 'son of Toll's son', i.e., father and *two*
sons – the Spirit is missing!

like the Jews if they were right and proper. What they fail to see is that they are too fond of themselves, and that they have an interest which causes them to dislike Jews; others like these same Jews as a result of some interest of theirs, and they themselves begin to like them once they acquire a different interest. Society's actual practice gives Jews a good report, and history gives them the best report of all other people; Jews, who are supposed to be particularly evil, history pronounces to have exercised the most potent ethical influence. There is no path leading from the 'ethical genius among the nations' to the 'community of the less gifted and the characterless,' and we cannot get away from the fact that Christ was a Jew. It is a fact that Christ was a Jew; Shylock, however, is an invention. Moreover Shylock is a made-up figure of a non-Jew, only subsequently applied to Jews.

But even if all Jews were Christs, they would be generally regarded the same as if they were all Shylocks. People at large are not just, but unjust, and they contribute to the triumph of the anti-Semites' injustice. Antisemitism bases its hatred on its unjust interest-judgment, which causes it to see nothing of the facts; it bases its hopes and prospects on the lack of thinking and lack of interest on the part of the public, which lacks even the interest to bring the facts to bear on that judgment which, not even seeing the real facts, believes the most unbelievable things about Jews.

It believes the Jews capable of plotting and carrying out the most inhuman and world-destroying things, both secretly and publicly. These things arise where one would least expect them, from people who, for the rest, do not think at all antisemitically, who think antisemitically as little as the fettered mediums of the spiritists have freedom of movement in their compartments, and yet they become the most amazing things in the air: potatoes, musical instruments, old bones. No less amazing are the fabulous horror stories about Jews believed in, and occasionally expressed, by people who have no interest whatsoever in antisemitism, even though such notions fly in the face of all that is real and possible, all likelihood and experience. But of such people is the public composed; they do not think genuinely critically. They do not confront the antisemitic judgment with the facts as society really experiences them nor with the facts of history; and as far as the latter are concerned they only know them in an unsatisfactory and mutilated form. They are not governed by the facts and their interconnections, nor by the achievements which they use to their own advantage: when their interest is eventually aroused, they range themselves against the Jews (and this is what the anti-Semites ultimately hope for and look for), imitating the anti-Semites and judging in the same way as they do. When it comes down to it, the generality of men judge in a truly astonishing way.

Indeed, how could a non-thinking society perpetrate anything else but nonsense and mischief? How can those whose thought is not motivated by an interest in thinking, but by the thoughts which arise from interest – how can they think anything other than absurdities? How can they avoid coming to grief on Cape Nonsense? In truth, society thinks, judges and condemns people by their Jewish names and noses! Because of the Jewish names and noses Jews become 'the others'; they are no longer seen as individuals like the individuals in the society of honourable people, where this or that one 'does' something. When a Jew has 'done' something, it is 'one of the others' who has done it. This is the heart of the whole matter, and it is equally as significant as the injustice of seeing Jews not as individuals but as 'the others', all alike. They do not belong to honourable society, they are not individuals, they do not even belong to the human race – 'there are human beings and there are Jews' – all Jews are to be regarded as *one* man, who is not a man: the Jews are Shylocks. This is proved by their iniquitous noses and names. If a Jew has no 'Jewish nose', he will have a Jewish name; we live in a coarse, plebeian world of words and names, where unpopular names bring misfortune. In the middle ages, when people were being tortured, it was those with 'bad' names who were put on the rack first, and so it is always the Jews with their Jewish names who are tortured first, and then come the other Jews – who bear the Jewish name 'Jew'. For the Jew is always called by a Jewish name, even if his name is not Jewish.

Every other man has one name and no more, but the Jew has
one name more than he has, the most Jewish name, the most
antisemitic insult: Jew. This hands him over to the pride of
others; it means not only that arrogance can pour contempt on
some despicable Jewish good-for-nothing: every non-Jewish
good-for-nothing, however despicable, can despise all Jews,
including the most honourable ones. A Jew may have the
greatest expert knowledge in matters of supreme importance,
he may have a sound and refined judgment, he may have a
pure heart full of noble love and the most fruitful and
miraculous thoughts, the kind of person who will bequeath his
name to the world: if he is still alive, once he is known to be a
'Jew', he must pack his bags and leave in disgrace. If it had
been known in advance that he was a Jew, he would not have
been allowed to unpack in the first place. And what is his most
sublime deed? – providing breakfast for pride. Where is there
a more effective spell than this word 'Jew'? It does not affect
everyone and at all times with the same, sure power as it does
the anti-Semite, but it does not entirely forfeit its power in
anyone (excepting those who have a particular interest in the
Jews), and a time may come when all will join forces with life
and soul against the Jews. Fundamentally all are anti-Semites;
the only real non-anti-Semites are the Jews, and, unlike their
friends, they are not kept away from antisemitism by an
interest that is, after all, fortuitous, but by their very nature and
by the primary interest of their life.

Fundamentally, therefore, there are really only Jews and anti-Semites; thus we perceive the state of the society through which antisemitism becomes powerful, because society itself is at root antisemitic, or potentially so. It is certainly not just; not even when it has no interest in being unjust. Haman wants to bring ruin on the Jews, and the King lends his power to the purpose; then, however, comes the beautiful Esther and the King saves the Jews – out of interest in justice. But the King is always the same, and Haman is always there, and there is not always a beautiful Esther to prompt the King's justice; and generally the Hamans can do whatever they like without fear of the gallows.

7.

SOCIETY DOES NOT THINK, IT ONLY IMPLEMENTS ITS INTERESTS

Having attained clarity about the nature of the (pride-related) judgments of men, of egoists – for these judgments are governed by practical egoism and egoistic-moralistic criticism – we have also become clear about the anti-Semites' judgment on Jews. For, if all human beings are egoists, following their interest or supposed interest, if it is impossible for them to be anything other than egoists, we can see that anti-Semites, with their judgment, are the blindest, the most dubious and dangerous egoists. Let us say it again: human beings must be egoists, they must think on the basis of their interest, and it is impossible for them to think in terms of justice. For human beings are things in motion in the world's constant movement, and their thought is the inner dimension of their motion; it is their feeling, knowing and willing. And since they can do no other than feel, know and will their interest, whence should they acquire the ability to feel, know and will justice? Motives come solely from the world of motion, and serve our practical interests; as for justice, it cannot even be grasped properly in theory. Plato rightly complains that, while everyone has the same ideas in the case of the word 'iron' or 'silver', all disagree when it comes to what is right and just and are at a loss as to how to express themselves coherently.

All human beings are egoists since their human-thingly, relative consciousness corresponds to their interest-oriented thinking, and the latter coincides with their human thingliness. As such, therefore, this human thingliness, including its relative consciousness, is no different from the thingliness of a stone. For the stone, too, is not at rest, but presses on what lies below it; man does not keep to himself with his egoistic, relative consciousness: he reaches all around him as if *his* rights were infinite, and abuses *rights*, the rights of all others. (The definitions of what is right and just converge, more or less, on the balance of rights, the equal validity of the subjects of rights – making no distinctions as to persons – and on the *suum cuique*.) Every man, however, abuses rights in his own interest as much as he can; ultimately he is only concerned with what is just and good to *him*, and no one is prepared to roast in hell for someone else. All men are egoists in this way. But there are two kinds of egoists among them who are utterly insufferable: the egoists without work, and the proud egoists. The egoists who want to eat but do not want to work, criminals, swindlers and certain modern aesthetes, are dangerous and dubious to a lesser extent as regards individual human beings, those round them and in their immediate circle; they are insufferable because, in the world of egoism, there is no reason why those who work should pay for the indolence and pleasure of the others. As for the egoists who judge on the basis of their pride-interest, however, who are determined that others should burn in hell for their pride, they are dangerous beyond measure; under certain circumstances they constitute a danger to the whole of society. We have seen that a special form of this highly dangerous pride-interest is antisemitism with its judgment on Jews. The anti-Semites' judgments do not merit the word 'judgment' at all as it is ordinarily used – although, as we have shown, the ordinary usage is itself illegitimate; their judgments are judgments based on interest, interests over which genuine judgments and thoughts have no power. Only interest can influence interest; thus the interest in thinking, in those who possess it, can have an influence over their interest-related thought. Only in such people to whom thought has done violence, through whom it surges, freely proceeding against interest, and in whom the interest in thinking is stronger than interest-related thought, can interest be pushed back and the truth come out. This means that it is impossible to speak to anti-Semites about what we have discussed here, about the essence of antisemitism and the genuine cause behind this effect, since one can only speak of the essences of things to people who think; naturally the latter can also think about human beings and come to grips with causes and effects. But as for anti-Semites being thinkers – well, it would not be calling white 'black' or dragging the sublime in the dust to say that anti-Semites do not bear the stamp of thought on their foreheads and that they generally use their heads only to rationalize their interests. Thinking would only be a hindrance in antisemitism, let alone thinking about Jews. In no case can they think of Jews as human beings; they can only inveigh against them as if they were not human beings. The utterances of anti-Semites on the slaughtering of Jews, e.g., in the last Russian pogroms (and so far we know of 40,000 killed and 100,00 wounded), do not really sound like statements about the slaughter of human beings, and in antisemitic books people quite seriously raise the question, whether Jews should be regarded as human. 'There are human beings, and there are Jews', say the German haters of Jews, and in doing so they show themselves just as superior to crude nature, which, with its stupid hands, has made Jews into human beings.

When these anti-Semites hear of the slaughter of Jews, they do not turn a hair or show the least trace of compassion: their thought does not exhibit a single trace of egoistic interest, i.e., they evince no fear that what has happened to the Jews might also happen to them. They are human beings: how can what happened to the Jews, happen to them?! They do not speak like human beings about other human beings, but like human beings about Jews. And what they think, in their healthy, comfortable bodies, about the slaughtering of Jews, is not the interest of compassion but of delight, of sadistic pleasure, of pleasure in the torments of those they hate. It really sounds like hatred of human beings – or have people forgotten, when it comes to hating Jews, what hatred of humans is? And when the anti-Semites ask whether Jews are human beings, does this mean that hatred of Jews is any less hatred of human beings, or is it, for that very reason, the most poisonous hatred of human beings? At all events they take it for granted that, if Jews are to be regarded as human beings, they are the very worst of the species, in no way to be compared to the anti-Semites with their human kindness.

People who understand nothing but inane invective against others, against whole groups of humanity, understand nothing about the human being; they do not think. Anti-Semites, because they give the most abuse, are among the human beings who think least, the utterly rank egoists who are totally barred from all insight into their own nature.

The saying, 'Know thyself' is ultimately addressed to the anti-Semites, not at all to ordinary people with nothing but egoistic interest; against the latter neither Enlightenment nor the Tree of Knowledge can do anything. Do not believe the fable; men still do not know the difference between good and evil, only what tastes good to them and what they covet; that is all they are in a position to address their thoughts to. Enlightenment is to no avail, least of all where antisemitism is concerned. One must not believe every fable, including the one which says that if a mirror is held up to a basilisk, it kills itself with its own poisonous stare.

The anti-Semites will not give up their antisemitism, nor do they understand it, since they do not think, but only engage in invective. Similarly, the Jews who can only hurl abuse at antisemitism do not understand its nature; they simply abuse the anti-Semites just as the latter abuse the Jews. They do this on the basis of egoistic interests, merely giving back the insults and calumnies which have been applied to them. Invective arising from egoistic interests is anything but thinking. (This is not to say anything against the exalted reproaches uttered by great spiritual men. No one does this more than Christ – but not from egoistic interest in honour or from envy of possession, of a higher standard of living, not from pride and jealousy; he attacks men's twisted egoism, and does so as a result of his reflection on eternal things, out of love and out of thought's anger at unthinking humanity, which, in his language, he calls 'sinful.' This is truth's magnificent reproach in the mouth of the man who could say, not, 'I bring you truth,' but, 'I am the truth!'). Anyone who, as an anti-Semite, abuses the Jews, does not think about antisemitism and does not understand anything of its essence; similarly, the Jew who utters vituperation against antisemitism does not think about it or understand it; and as for the person who stands half-way between the two forms of abuse, he does not think or understand either. All these attacks and half-hearted attacks are simply beating the air. Only in ideas, such as are developed here, do we have firm ground and reality; this is the first and last word concerning antisemitism. (It is also my last word on antisemitism, for after this book I shall be once again both ex-Judaeus and ex-politicus, as before, and will no longer torment myself with these most hideous and inane things; I shall take up my own, far more beautiful chapter again.) This is the only word germane to antisemitism – all the rest is blatant interest and babbling; this is the only way to move forward.

It is just not possible, whether with or without verbal abuse, to overthrow antisemitism by thought, by each person individually invoking justice, here, there and everywhere. The anti-Semites may consider themselves moral and just: I think they are not; the Jews may consider themselves moral and just: I think they are not.

And both anti-Semites and Jews may consider me to be unjust and immoral; both of them may be annoyed because I regard them both as human beings and consider no man to be moral and just. I have looked very closely at man, and have found as little morality or suchlike in man as in steam or electricity, and a man is no more just towards other men than an animal or a stone is. There is not a trace of anything moral or just in man's egoism: there are motives that arise from the dark regions of his mind, anxieties, cowardice, twisted ideas, and the superstition which all these produce, but this is not morality. Anyone speaking of human affairs should leave alone notions of morality in the accepted sense, as well as justice and thinking. The words, thinking, justice and morality have not the slightest meaning in human affairs; men could just as well use the words 'baa', 'gigshumla' and 'bluffsaui' instead. Am I mocking justice when I say that justice is not-injustice? Justice is a daughter of heaven, it is heaven itself; justice, beautiful, great and radiant, has never left heaven. But Satan was cast out of heaven and thrown upon the earth. Injustice, the vile colossus of Satan, stalks all over the earth and makes our entire earth filthy, and wherever he puts his hideous feet, now here, now there, our life dies between them. Or, without using metaphor and mythology: justice and thought are not found among men and in the world: men do not think, they are animals. They are not wicked, but treat each other wickedly, and do not live as brothers and sisters (and even brothers and sisters do not always live thus) or as comrades.

In fact, justice and thought only exist in mythology: the angels treat each other as comrades, for hostility has no place among them, nor envy or hatred or quarrelsome talk (Cant. r. f. 34b). What man knows anything of justice but the man who suffers injustice? And as for the justice and the rights they deal in, what are they but their continual self-righteousness or their self-seeking? 'Where justice is, no people dwell.' Men do not have the interest of justice or the interest of thought; devoid of spirit, the only thinking they have is that of egoistic interest and of injustice – i.e., not injustice as a mere breach in an otherwise continuous justice, either. They should no longer pretend that they possess *justitia originalis*, as before the Fall.

It is all interest, nothing but interest, never leading to justice, but very often to injustice. This characterizes the essence of human society. It is important to recognize this if one wants to speak to human society about its essence in a way that is really profitable. Either society thinks, and thus grasps the way its own nature is constructed, or it is assuredly condemned to perpetrate the same injustices for all time. (And to achieve this understanding it must cling to reality and the knowledge of reality, to philosophy, and give up blathering scholasticism, particularly that of Immanuel Kant with his categorically imperative moral law which addresses man, independent of any egoistic interest; this is refuted by a single opponent: the human race.) Either society thinks or injustice will persevere forever; *anything one thinks wrongly necessarily is lived wrongly.**

---

* Italized by Editor.

All the chit-chat about justice, all this asking the wolf not to devour the sheep, is as foolish as it is dangerous. The more it believes in the succour of justice, the more it is hindered from helping itself by improving the conditions for life and thus diminishing the danger threatening it. The way to improve conditions is not, as formerly, by linking interest to moralism (for in that case people will only dissimulate on the stage of moralism and simply hide their interest, however unjust it may be; they will never give it up), but by linking what is just to a greater interest than that which injustice has for them. Otherwise there will be no improvement. *And that is why nothing is improved* – nothing in the entire picture; for every individual improvement there is some other individual deterioration – and so the situation remains dire, just as it always has been, because unthinking society does not understand and it is impossible to show it its essence, its real nature, whence all these things come. For this is why all men are in conflict with one another and produce verdicts upon each other, why the human being is actually only good within very narrow limits, outside of which he becomes evil for others and for ourselves, the worst danger and scourge threatening mankind – this is not regarded as the kind of talk likely to lead to a grasp of the subject, and the *animalia disputantia* are not heard debating on this essential point.

They are not interested in it; it is not their interest it is only the truth about what interests them. They simply do not listen if one tries to say, 'This is what you should think, if you want to think – and unless you think in these terms you will be renouncing thought altogether – namely, quite simply: there is love, the possession-interest, the prestige-interest, honour-vanity and pride, and the falsification of judgment as a result of these interests. This is the conclusive description of the human being; this makes everything clear and solid, particularly when you start to appreciate the prestige-interest in its full significance, distinguishing it from its disguises and realizing that most of the world's anger, rage, hatred and revenge result from it. But as for your nonentities, like justice and your frail, bent concepts and your many words which are not rooted in these simple factors and cannot hold reality fast, they have led you astray completely: reality escapes you, you become only confused, quite blind in your interests, and you yourselves increase the danger you are in.' In their view all this says nothing, whereas in fact it says everything. In our case as in every other case. What is unessential, what is not genuine thought at all but merely interest, is taken for thought and speech. It is your fault – no, it is your fault! – this is the dogmatic terminology of their superstition which they apply to one another; this is the way they conduct their controversies; this is the way they imagine they can understand and think. These are sturdy intelligibilities with which to thrash each

other and avoid using their heads to think. Mutual thrashing is
not the way to think and find the truth!

8.

HATE: SOMA & PSYCHE, SPINOZA'S DEFINITION

As far as every person who really thinks is concerned,
anti-semitism is judged and condemned; for that very reason it
remains the property of non-thinking society, which possesses
nothing but its inert interest-related thinking and its pride-
dominated moral criticism, a society which, contrary to all
justice, stands all facts on their heads for the sake of its interest
and pride. This is just what the anti-Semites do on the basis of
their anti-Jewish interest, which eventually becomes an insane
preoccupation. In doing so, as we have seen, they are no
longer against the Jews but against the facts. The antisemitic
judgment is refuted if we take a transverse section of our
society and a longitudinal section through our history. Anti-
Semites are people who promote Judaism by tormenting Jews.
I have already said that without antisemitism both Jews and
Judaism would come to an end; and one anti-Semite less for
the Jews would mean one Jew less for the world. This is true:
Haman did more for the Jews than all the prophets taken
together. What the prophets could not do, anti-Semites have
achieved: they have made Jews and Judaism everlasting.

However, these meritorious executioners do not play an
attractive role on this account; nor are they to be held in high
honour.

For by keeping hatred of Jews alive, they keep hatred of human beings alive too; and there can be nothing more execrable, for the human race, than hatred of human beings. Hatred of human beings makes man into a despicable animal, specifically human. For the other animals all do better than we animals do: they act towards each other as animals, but man acts inhumanly towards man. It is a slander on the other animals to call this hate, which keeps emerging in man, 'bestial'. It is only in man that this hate constantly arises; consequently, with his hate that comes from pride and an *interest that does not spring from necessity*, man is worse than the beast of prey, which is innocent. Man is therefore the beast who hates, intrinsically the malicious animal of destruction. This needs to be said today more than ever; far more than in earlier times, humanity needs to be reminded of its non-thinking, its worthless traits and sins, for today it seems to be more than ever entangled in them *in diabolical pride*. Now that humanity has once again been totally swallowed up in its worldly and thingly nature, it is high time to preach true Judaism, i.e., true Christianity, to it, in order to steer a few people – even if not the whole of humanity – away from this vice of pride, compared with which I am prepared to sing the praises of all the other vices. Men must be steered away from the pride of their spiritual and intellectual impoverishment which arises as a result of materialistic education, from their being engrossed in pride in their science and technology, and from their pride versus one another, from their absolute bestialization, i.e., from the absolutizing of their animal nature, their narrowness, their worthlessness, their wretchedness, their abominations committed with shining eyes. We must do this, above all, *for the sake of those who are capable of thinking and who suffer under diabolical pride and hatred, to give them at least, clarity, renewal and strength.* Nowadays the hatred of human beings is celebrating victories as probably never before in the history of the human race; there has surely never been such *incitement* to hatred as there is now. Since people do not think, but only have an interest that only too easily gets out of control, and are always inclined to mount the horse of pride and become judge and executioner of their dear neighbours – and they are good at it – we can understand what incitement means among human beings: everyone can experience it for himself (at least if he finds himself being thus incited). And in general, as we have said, there has never been such incitement to hatred of human beings as there is at present. Hatred of human beings; this is what it is, though it may seek to hide behind lofty-sounding names, as if it were something other than hatred of human beings. But it *is*, it *is*, it *is*, hatred of human beings, and people ought to talk a great deal about it, and not keep quiet and let it hide away like that, since it is the most baneful, the only really dangerous hatred of man. For hatred on the part of individuals as a result of bitter disappointment and hurt is an extremely rare and temporary pathological condition of the soul; it is recognized and treated as a pathological condition, and usually manifests a contemplative character. Moralism is to blame for it: it is a melancholic brooding on corrupt human nature, and enough has been said about the latter on the basis of moralism without compounding it with melancholy as well, as, for instance, the man who said: 'Anyone who, in his fortieth year, does not hate human beings, has never loved them.' The hatred of human beings of which we speak, however, with its exclusively active character which society by no means sees as a sickness, and its monstrous gluttony which causes society no concern whatsoever, this real hatred of human beings, rooted in human nature, could assuredly make the thinker – who is devoid of moralism – into an individual hater of men, if he were not too healthy precisely because he is a thinker and impervious to all hatred (not least because he cannot consider any man to be the free cause of his actions). For this hatred of human beings points to non-thinking and what is fundamentally evil in humanity, originating in pride and group pride.

It is a total lack of self-knowledge that leads to this pride and group pride which despises, ridicules, curses and hates human nature – as it is found in other human beings; this is what leads to this most hateful passion which, unlike the other passions, never comes to an end and wanes, and, in tormenting the object of hatred, also torments the hater himself. Do you know which of the two is the more tormented, the hated or the hater?! Envy, vexation, violent loathing, and the fact that he is often disappointed in his hopes of revenge –

all this torments the hater; and he is always tormented by the thought that he does not torment his quarry enough. It is not enough for him to flee from all communion with the object of his hatred (the word hate has been connected with χᾶσις , separation: *quia odium est affectus dispunctionis*): he feels a passionate compulsion to banish the one he hates from all communion with other human beings, to banish him for ever; he must even spew his poison into the hearts of children. The hater torments because he himself is tormented; for hatred is no less active in the body of the hater than love in the body of the lover. Even anger itself stimulates the action of the heart and the circulation of the blood; the arteries swell and the person blushes with anger: but the one who hates is really sick, an evil wine has mixed with his blood, his blood *boils within him for very hatred*. He does not succeed, by tormenting the object of his hatred, in assuaging his own torment, which ceaselessly renews itself like the thirst of one sick with fever. No humiliation, no misery on the part of the hated is sufficient – he would like to eradicate him utterly; and even this is not enough: he would like to be sure that the person he hates is enduring the tortures of eternal damnation. *This* was real hatred: a man followed and stalked his victim for years, and often had a chance to strike him down, but held off until he had the unfortunate man completely in his power. He threatened him with death unless he would forswear his eternal bliss; and when the latter, in abject fear, actually forswore it, *then he murdered him!*

The hater *can* be a blood-murderer: he *must* always seek to murder the honour of the one he hates. Christ says that the person who hates is guilty of murder. If the world only understood why Christ calls the hater a murderer! This is how Christ understood it, as Luther rightly says: 'Do you think he was only talking about your fist when he says, Thou shalt not kill!? What does he mean by *thou*? Not merely your hand, nor your foot, nor your tongue, nor any other member, but *all that you are in body and soul*. Just as if I say to someone, You should not do that, I am not speaking with my fist but with my whole person. Indeed, even if I put it like this: Your hand should not do it, I do not mean the hand alone but the whole human being to which the fist belongs. For the hand itself would do nothing unless the whole body with all its members acted in concert. So when he says, Thou shalt not kill, it is as much as if he said: however many members you may have, and however many ways you may find to kill, whether with your hand, tongue, heart, or by signs and gestures, by looking hostile and using your eyes to begrudge this person his life, or by using your ears against him by not wanting to hear him spoken of. All this is killing: for your heart and all that is in you inclines to wish him dead. And although, for the present, your hand keeps still, your tongue is silent, and your eyes and ears hide themselves, your heart is still full of murder and slaughter.'

If only the world could look into its own heart and see hatred and itself in this way, and understand that those who kill with their hands are not so dangerous – for there are few of them – and do not do so much killing as those who do not kill with their hands! This is Christ's great truth concerning men: 'Why do you talk about the few sinners you call sinners? I will talk to you about something really terrible; *your* sinfulness, *the sinfulness of you all!'* This is something extraordinary and unique, and Christ taught it and lived it as no other ever did: he never inveighs against the sinfulness of those called 'sinners' by others, but only and always against the sinfulness of all. He keeps company with the simple and with sinners, with tax-collectors and harlots; he cannot stand the others, the proud haters, the entire society of respectable people. Pride and hatred play a very great role in society and create baneful separation between people; Christ lives in the realm of the spirit and of love, which is not a realm of separation but the realm of the ONE, and no one is further from this than the hater. For the hater, in the untruth and wretchedness of his abhorrence-ridden consciousness, imagines himself to be at a furthest remove from the object of his hatred, whereas in fact he is one with it in the ONE. This is the immeasurable scale of his passion and his misery: with his active denial he is intent on creating dissension and destruction within the unity, whereas it is he who is astray, his mind is beclouded and incapable of genuine reflection; in his blind raging he knows nothing but the unruly, intrinsically heinous bestial interest. Thinking that he hates 'the other', he is in reality a self-hater, he hates his own eternal being, the being of the absolute Eternal Spirit which, in his relativity, he always carries with him, even if he lacks the sacred consciousness of it. The hater lacks spirit; he is spiritless, spiritless in all his utterances – just as, conversely, Christ is always in the Spirit, and love is always eloquent in him.

No one listens to Christ. They make the most nonsensical and superstitious use of his teaching on the sinfulness of all men, creating obligations that drive men mad and to sins that arise from madness, and all the time they hold on to their pride and hatred. Nothing of this Jew's 'religion of love' has been implemented in the world; the chief result it achieved was hatred of Jews. Were Jews ever meant to hear of his love? Love cannot be proclaimed with the sound of drums, as hatred can, nor does it bind as many people together as the latter. Today, once again, the drums are uttering hatred, making more noise than ever – thus we can again identify a significant surge of civilization. Once more the drums are proclaiming hatred of Jews, which is in fact hatred of the human race, a genuine hatred, similar to that of the hater to whom we have already referred. For, as far as the hatred of Jews is concerned, no humiliation of Jews would be sufficiently abject, even if the Jews were prepared to say: 'All right, we will not aspire to become officers and judges; we will no longer be lawyers and doctors; we will never again excel in any branch of science, art or philosophy; we will creep away into the ghetto; and – oh yes, yes – Christianity was made by Christians, who were not Jews, and – yes, yes – Jesus Christ was not a Jew but a Saxon anti-Semite.' This would still not be enough for the hatred of Jews for it would only signify civil death. Hatred of Jews is more than mortal hatred: it is hellish hatred; and civil death is not enough unless this civil death also entails civil hell.

Hatred of Jews is truly hatred of human beings, even if it is called antisemitism. Do not let a word deceive you. And should you not be ashamed to find that you have become indifferent towards something which, seen for what it is, cannot but be utterly detested? Or, if you no longer recognize hatred as hatred and no longer understand what hatred is, let the philosopher tell you, *the* philosopher, Spinoza (for anyone who knows how to distinguish living philosophical truth from scholastic chaff also knows that Spinoza is *the* philosopher and that he has the same individual, unique significance in philosophy as Shakespeare has in literature, Michelangelo in sculpture and Beethoven in music). 'Hatred,' writes Spinoza, 'is displeasure, combined with the imaginary external cause of this displeasure. The hater strives to remove and destroy the hated object. He feels pleasure in imagining the object of his hatred to be experiencing displeasure or destruction.

If he imagines someone giving pleasure to some object which he hates, he will be stirred up to hatred of that person as well; and conversely, if he imagines someone inflicting displeasure on the hated object, he will be stirred up to love of that person. Moreover, he strives to affirm every displeasure he imagines to be inflicted upon him by the object of his hatred, and to deny every pleasure he imagines to be attributable to the hated object. He will have an unjustly small opinion of the object of his hatred, just as he has an unjustly large opinion of himself and of the object of his love. (This is pride and a kind of insanity – he regards all the products of his imagination as reality, and inflates himself on that account.) Furthermore the hater will strive, as far as he can, to make everyone hate whatever he himself hates. However, all the emotions of hatred, namely, envy, derision, contempt, anger, revenge, and the other emotions that relate to hatred or spring from it, are evil; all that we do under the influence of hatred is dishonourable; in terms of the state, it is unjust.' In these words of Spinoza we have the classical description of hate in general. It is with this same hate that the Jews are hated by the Jew-haters and anti-Semites. In these following sentences Spinoza doubtless had the hatred of Jews particularly in mind: 'If anyone is moved to displeasure by the member of another class or nation, and thinks of him – under the general heading of his class or nation – as the cause, he will hate not only him but all the members of his class or nation.

As a result of the similarity with the object which first aroused the emotion of hatred, this hatred will be elicited afresh'. (*Der Judenhass und die Juden*, p. 96, 97; 3rd. ed.).

Believe this: beneath their skin, anti-Semites are Jew-haters. Jews cannot be worse hated, indeed, human beings cannot be worse hated by other human beings than by anti-Semites. What more can hate achieve than this antisemitic revulsion against Jewish persons, against all their manifestations, utterances, endeavours, and ideas? It goes to the lengths of utter contradiction: if a Jew's view on some particular subject coincides with that of an anti-Semite, the latter will immediately take the opposite view. What more can hate achieve than this envy and this delight in harm? For as long as things do not go badly for the Jews, all the anti-Semites' delights are soaked in vinegar. What more can hate achieve than this calumny, enmity, malice, desire for revenge and, where it can get away with it, acts of hostility and annihilation – blind, vicious, poisonous, deadly, hellish hate!

Antisemitism is hatred of Jews; and the Jews and those who have defended them committed a grave tactical error by using the word antisemitism instead of 'hatred of Jews'. They did not have to allow this usage, given their power over the press – for the 'Jewish press' too can create a deathly silence around real live human beings, at least for a short time (i.e., during their lifetime) – with their power over the press and the literary world they could have prevented it taking root.

This is a case where the modern fad for scientific-sounding names has become really dangerous – and, in general, thinking is gravely threatened due to the fact that language is more and more removed from the plain reference; it is often the case that, in words of the highest importance, there is no direct expression of the actual, objective meaning. The expression, 'hatred of Jews', honestly announces its meaning; there can be no question of its referring, perhaps, to something praiseworthy or even decent in the human being. Hatred of Jews is hatred of human beings, and the expression 'hatred of Jews' will not allow us to stray very far from this meaning. But adopt another word for the evil thing and the evil thing dons a mask; this signifies barefaced attack on the very language which renders things intelligible to us. The word 'antisemitism' draws the verdict on hatred of Jews away from the line which, at all costs, it ought to hold: it shifts the standpoint out of what is plainly human and into the obscure area of an opposition which, by the use of this scientific-sounding word, seems to acquire some justification.

Words are of infinite benefit and do infinite harm; they are men's chief aid, but they are also pre-eminent in introducing confusion among men. Non-thinking people are happy enough when they are only babbling, but they lose their heads entirely over high-sounding words and names, which totally separate them from the concept's content and from logic; as a result, ultimately, they actually think using other means than logic, as for instance in theo-logic. The latter taught them to worship cats and crocodiles and, finally, even the absolute Nothing as the Thing of Things, the God which would help them to get to a fairytale life in the sky. The belief in this was assuredly the most ridiculous self-conceit of human pride, which then turned into the most monstrous chimera, each man hating and persecuting the other for not having the same view of the ultimate absurdities as he had. The other animals are spared this folly of men not least because they do not speak in words and names – *O that mankind could hold its peace for three generations!* What have men not thought and done in the Name of Names, Amen; how ridiculous they have made themselves, and what monstrous deeds they have perpetrated! Words can do everything with men. If, instead of the word 'murderer', for instance, the word 'antibiotician' (or some equally serviceable barbarism) were to become accepted usage, I am certain that the safety of our lives would soon be in jeopardy.

Words have performed the most marvellous service, particularly in the deception practised against the Jews: we have already seen this in the case of the word 'Jew' itself and the word 'Christianity', and now we have the word 'antisemitism' as a respectable lid covering the shameful hatred of Jews. 'Antisemitism, what kind of a thing is that?' O, it is something miraculous, a most singular word of enchantment, making things different, and yet they stay as they are. The word changes, and the world is changed. The word 'antisemitism' is different from 'hatred of Jews', so antisemitism must be different from hatred of Jews; so, in turn, hatred of Jews is different from hatred of Jews and from hatred of human beings. Particularly since it shows itself as something else in those who hate, and nature has not branded the word 'man-hater' on their foreheads; moreover, hatred of human beings is not something horribly alien to men: it does not breathe an icy frost over loving hearts, as if they were bound to die from it. Only for Jews is antisemitism nothing other than hatred of Jews, hatred of human beings, making them hated men. They must fight; they ought also to fight for this word 'hatred of Jews'; it is part of their fight for their rights. And the hatred of Jews has a right to be called by its name; otherwise it will fail to recognize itself. The most abominable human infamy must not, gradually and by subterfuge, lose its name as the most abominable human infamy. It is the duty of Jews, of their friends and of all thinking people, and particularly, of course, of thinking Jews, to be vigilant about this. And since the word 'antisemitism' can no longer be completely avoided now, people must at least be reminded, sufficiently emphatically and often, of its straightforward translation; we do not intend to forget how to speak plain German.

9.

SUMMARY, RETROSPECT AND PROSPECTS

Jews must suffer injustice, that is, the evil effects of hatred of Jews. Contrary to what the Jew-haters maintain and think they have demonstrated with their alleged proofs, the Jews are not the cause of this hatred. Jews are not the cause, but the target, of the hatred of Jews, and it is erroneous to see Jews and the hatred of Jews in the relationship of cause and effect.

Without entering into the details of all the accusations and defences, all the arguments pro and contra, which cannot produce a decision, we have presented incontrovertible and self-evident proofs with regard to the influence exerted by Jews. A comparison of the influences alleged by anti-Semites and the quite different and contrary influences attested by the facts showed us this: that Jews simply cannot be the cause of hatred of Jews. However, we did not idly leave it at that; we were by no means content to let the effect, i.e., hatred of Jews, stand in isolation, without a cause. We have seen from the birth certificate of the hatred of Jews that it originates in pride; we have identified the real cause of hatred of Jews in the interest-dominated judgment of pride, which is blind to all humanity, reason and fact; and furthermore we have found that the Jews are the circumstantial cause in the emergence of the hatred of Jews. The poison which hatred of Jews represents is not produced by Jews: it is the poison of arrogance in the Jew-haters themselves. As for the existence of Jews, it is the condition under which this poison ferments in them. When the circumstantial cause (the Jews) accompanies the actual cause (pride), the Jew-haters take the circumstance to be the actual cause. This is so because no one recognizes his arrogance as pride and as the cause of ill; in general, the more remote cause of some effect is not so easily discovered, and this is even more so in this case, since the cause seems to lie so near at hand (i.e., the Jews seem to be this cause). Thus the Jew-haters and others too, those who are leaders and those who are led astray, regard what is the catalyst as the actual cause.

Our task has therefore been completed, since all effects have been traced back to their causes (for here, as everywhere, the difficulty is to find one's way to the causes and effects that really belong to each other) and, by confronting the counter-proofs, we have clearly exposed antisemitism in its absurdity. In face of the contribution Jews have made to society and history, the judgment of the anti-Semites, namely, that Jews are inferior and morally degenerate, sounds neither like a judgment of history nor like a divine judgment, but more like the idea of a quadrangular circle. A circle is round, and the anti-Semite who talks about a quadrangular circle is talking nonsense. Quite contrary to the assertion of the anti-Semites,

it would be far more germane to ask whether the Jews must
not be credited with a pre-eminent talent, if not in the realm of
the intellect also, then at least in the ethical realm; we should
ask whether it is not among the Jews, more than among other
people, that there is to be found that love and justice which the
Jews alone have announced to the rest of mankind.

Whether this is a fact or not (and I do not believe that it
is[1]) will be difficult to decide as long as Jews live their lives as

---

[1] Many do believe this, and they even believe that Jews are intellectually
more talented. Of the more recent statements to this effect let us quote what
Pastor Steudel writes in his *Deutscher Geist und Judenhass* pp. 115-116: 'Not
all envy is base. I personally have been long convinced, on the basis of my
studies going back as far as the Babylonian period of pre-history, and from
my lifelong preoccupation with the "sacred writings" of Jews and Christians,
as well as from history of civilization that reaches down to our day, that the
Semitic race is spiritually superior to the so-called Aryan. And as a German
I feel that there is something simply tragic about this conclusion. Every day I
meet not only with shrewd, far-seeing, uninhibited entrepreneurial
calculation, but also with artistic talent, the poetic treatment of form, and a
delicate sense of style, pre-eminently among Jews, Jews of mixed blood and
their descendants; and I sense that I am not free from a certain secret envy.
All the time I remain aware, however, that these excellences on the other
side are balanced by quite different excellences on our side. That is why I
can never see the solution of present difficulties in a hostile struggle against
Semitism, but solely in an honest debate between the two racially alien and
opposed parties, in which inadequacies would be openly admitted on both
sides. On our side we should admit to a certain lack of form, a certain
plodding sluggishness, a distrustful and hesitant attitude towards all new and
progressive ideas; the other side would have to admit a certain tendency to
allow the unrestrained nature of a volatile spirit to become distorted into
ethical unscrupulousness and the chaotic extravagances of artistic form. The
triumph of what is noble in nature and culture can only be found where
things that are mutually alien endeavour to profit through contact with each
other, and where balance is sought in a higher synthesis. This insight,
however, is opposed by today's antisemitism (which is to be explained in
terms of the resentment felt by the inferior) with a barbaric lack of
understanding. Those who cannot forget that the Semitic race created the
figure of Jesus and produced a Spinoza, will be aware that systematic and
violent quarantine measures against Semitic "infection" are bound to deprive
our culture of a supply of the noblest energies. Anyone who knows the
contribution which has demonstrably been made by Jews to the development
of our culture, also knows that to strangle the valuable fertilizing process that
comes from the Semitic side would be to condemn the progress of civilization
to come practically to a halt.'

an oppressed and persecuted group within the society of others. The latter, society as a whole, will never allow itself to be guided by love and justice. This corresponds to the nature of its consciousness, which does not permit it to think, but only to pursue its interest-related thought, bringing injustice, pride and hatred in its wake; it only promotes justice if by doing so it can satisfy some egoistical interest; and in such cases even Jew-haters start becoming just towards Jews and having some feeling towards them. We have already mentioned that, for instance, wanting to marry Miss Goldpenny is a human affection which even the anti-Semite shares. Hatred of Jews, open or latent – like the hatred of negroes and Armenians, but primarily the hatred against the Jews who, because of their achievements and historical position, enjoy such a high importance – this hatred, for those human beings who *think*, is an incomparable means of getting to know their own race and of discovering the true relationship, in the human race, between justice and intellectual judgments on the one hand, and interests on the other; it is the best means of bidding farewell to all idealistic phrases concerning the nature of this our race – as if it were advancing steadily on the legs of reason and justice. Thinking about hatred enables us to examine ourselves whenever we make a judgment, and ask ourselves whether it is not, perhaps, dominated by some improper interests of ours or some inherited wrong interest, in regard to which we and our consciences have not yet become free. For the thinking person, who, in his consciousness, distinguishes interest-bound thinking from that part of his thinking which really achieves cognition, can form valid judgments (because they are without egoistic interest) and possesses a real, firm, unerring knowledge, and thus his conscience ($\sigma \upsilon \nu \varepsilon \iota \delta \eta \sigma \iota \varsigma$!) is of the same order. In the hatred of Jews, in antisemitism, the best human beings have a means of deepening cognition, of purifying the emotions, of moderating the will and of steeling the character; in antisemitism we have the touchstone for society's condition. Antisemitism, in which the hatred of human beings is permanently manifest to the light of day, is nothing foreign to this society. Antisemitism is related to society at large in the same way that a storm is related to the rest of nature: we observe the electric effect primarily as it is manifested in the storm, but – as every electrifying machine shows – the whole of nature is electric. The anti-Semites are the exponents of that side of this society which is characterized by injustice, pride and hatred.

This is why, though it has emancipated Jews, society has been unable to show justice to them. The hope that emancipation, once it has been promulgated on the basis of universal principles of human and civil rights, can actually be implemented, is founded on a total misreading of this society and of human nature, which cannot *accustom* itself to what is just, any more than the Jews can accustom themselves to suffering injustice. No. It is not as simple as saying, 'There's the sickness, here's the cause – Right!' As we have seen, hatred of Jews is not to be regarded as a sickness at all.

For we have plenty of physicians who have invented powders against illness; how many infallible cures there are against every illness, so much so that it is inconceivable that illnesses can still strike people and hold them fast!

What we are faced with is not a sickness on the part of society, but society itself and its interest. So long as society has an interest in injustice, any justice that comes from above, imposed by state decree, remains powerless. Justice decreed by the state is too high above society's interests to have any influence on them: it is society, with its interest, with the prejudices and injustice of its interest, that has the decisive power; it entraps this justice by decree in its nets and brings about its ruin. This is legislation's great struggle against customary justice and customary injustice. Justice and humanness are powerless, and it is the same story with the triumph of knowledge and enlightenment. It is always interests that count, only interests. Anyone who wants to understand the human being only needs to consider the interests which are really there under his skin, not his external garments, his knowledge and his enlightenment, his stock of information and acquired patterns of thought (apart from the few who really feel the power of the interest in thinking, who really feel the spirit, both the learned and the unlearned have nothing but their interest). It is the same with the generality of men. The worthlessness of all enlightenment cannot be emphasized enough. No enlightenment concerning antisemitism is of any serious use, for it is antisemitism itself that needs enlightening. What is effective, on the contrary, is when people are 'enlightened' as to the wickedness of the Jews: this immediately acts as a spur to interest, the interest of possession and the interest of pride, since the lies which flatter pride have complete power over base minds. All enlightenment as to the wickedness of the Jews serves to arouse the urge to slander, to act insolently, to hate and persecute. Not least, it stimulates the need for some factor to which one's discontent can be attributed (which is why people whose discontent has a quite different cause, but who cannot vent their anger on it, join in thrashing the Jewish scapegoat: here they can vent their rage! And even people who are fundamentally content lend a hand and join in the thrashing). Just see how the wickedness of the Jews gets them going! When enlightenment is leading, however, they drag their heels behind it as if escorting a corpse to its eternal rest. That is why it is all up with the 'final triumph of enlightenment and justice'. Finitude lasts for eternity.

If there is any improvement for human society, with its intellectual and ethical endowment which is essentially constant throughout all ages, such improvement comes through a change in circumstances in society. This or that injustice loses popularity; the interest in it loses energy or dries up entirely; some new interest has emerged and society no longer has an interest in this or that injustice; it may even have acquired an interest in justice in some particular case. But as for justice for justice's sake, it does not exist and can never be attained through world process. In the life of the individual, as in the course of history, the most unexpected things happen, misfortune and fortune, reason and the ultimate unreason, but the expected justice never arrives, most certainly it does not. Justice for justice's sake may exist on paper and in words and in the good will, which does not understand itself at the time. Man has good will towards justice, but he does not love it; justice wanes with the passage of time, but the interest in advantage remains. Man and his advantage, once they have gazed into each other's eyes, cannot resist one another, they love each other. That straightway puts an end to all justice, which does not produce any egoistic advantage. No one can forcibly compel justice to be done to him, since *unusquisque tantum juris habet, quantum potentia valet*; even an acknowledged injustice in society is not done away with unless society also has some advantage in doing away with it. So it was over with the emancipation of the Jews, once it had come about: it did not result in justice in general towards Jews and only injustice towards a few anti-Semites at the same time. Emancipation was a case of that good will we have mentioned; it was a case of an acknowledged injustice, the abolition of which is not connected to any advantage. That is why it turns back again.

The injustice is less and less recognized, the better the will recognizes itself in what is its own and extracts itself from any entanglement with the 'good will' and the clichés connected with it. The good will becomes increasingly a bad will, injustice transforms itself once more into justice and the emancipation of the Jews seems to have been a misfortune or, at any rate, not a success. And yet its most courageous and enthusiastic protagonists would not have believed it possible, would not have dreamed that it could have succeeded in the way it has. They would have smiled at the prophecy that, a few generations after their emancipation, Germans of Jewish descent would be as distinguished as other Germans in philosophy, art, literature, science, technology, in all professions and in politics, and that they would be so German that no party in Germany would not have received its political programme from Germans of Jewish descent. This was not prophesied, but it has come about; now that it has come about, however, everything seems different from how it looks, and most people still believe as they did in the middle ages, that the Jews are to blame for all public misfortune, war and famine. In other words people have by no means progressed, let alone become enlightened, as a result of their 'progress' and 'enlightenment.' Jews are prevented from experiencing the whole range of persecutions undergone in the middle ages because of the changed conditions, not because men have changed. Men have not changed, the spirit of society has not changed; antisemitism has remained, with its logical and historical nonsense and its man-hating desecration of the human animal. Since society itself is the soil and root of antisemitism, the latter grows up again and once more has power and range over almost the whole of society. Now Jews have an edict that is full of justice, but a world full of injustice the same as before. The constant factor is this society's insincerity towards Jews; as far as possible they are still cheated of their honour.

Essentially Jews remain the race that has no honour. There are three things that could change this: the human character could be changed and improved, or Jews could acquire power to compel others to grant them their rights, or there could be a change and an improvement in society's external conditions. The first and second of these seem out of the question. As regards the third, the improvement of conditions, things have already improved for Jews and will continue to do so. (A further improvement of conditions would follow, as we have already suggested, from the punishment of the insults and calumnies commonly endured.)

This will continue to improve.... Emancipation set Jews the task of emancipating themselves from their isolation, and they confused this task with assimilation. Most people thought that the emancipation of the Jews meant their becoming assimilated to non-Jews; it was to be achieved in a flash while at the same time they had no idea what it meant, nor what is

involved in a long historical process; they ought to have known
at least what it is not and never can be, namely, justice towards
Jews.

The Jews themselves believed the same and thought
that emancipation meant justice and the fastest possible
assimilation.... Jews must extricate themselves from all the
wrong-headed notions of emancipation. The truth of
emancipation is not that the Jews are to be assimilated and
rendered indistinguishable from non-Jews, but that they should
be generally acknowledged by others in their distinctness, and
that they should appreciate their own authentic and specific
nature. Germans of Jewish descent should no more surrender
this specific nature than other Germans should give up theirs.[2]
Germans of Jewish decent should cultivate their specific
qualities while giving up all unnecessary differences. They
must not give up their specific nature. Their specific nature is
the same thing as their truthfulness and their naiveté.
Therefore they must surrender neither their specific nature nor
their truthfulness and sense of truth, their inner freedom and
their own self.

---

[2] 'Of course they also have their specific nature as Germans, but we must not
forget (and I constantly remind myself) that all Germans, indeed all human
beings, have their specific qualities. We found, did we not, that it is through
their specific qualities that individual human beings participate in life, and
through their specific qualities that groups of human beings participate in
national life; the wealth of specific natures gives rise to the development of
national life. As we saw, membership of the Jewish race no more prevents
people from being Germans than membership of the Germanic race prevents
people from being either German or English. The awareness of race and
nationality does not introduce a dichotomy into the individual. We have
agreed that the awareness of race belongs to the social sphere, which does
not stand in opposition to the political and national; indeed, a copulation of
the two is dangerous – thus the anti-Semites dance at the wedding of racial
awareness and national awareness and rejoice at the murderous child of this
marriage: strife.' (*Der Judenhass und die Juden* pp. 392-393.)

What is specific to them is their freedom and their self, which is why their being set free, in emancipation, means being acknowledged in their specific nature; and this emancipation, given the character of mankind and the position of Jews in society, will continue to be far less perfect for Jews than for other human beings. Nothing is clearer, once we understand human society and the equivocal status of Jews in this society and give up babbling about justice, humanity, enlightenment, etc. What is human society? All its members are supposed to live for one another, and yet they cannot live for one another without at the same time living in opposition to one another; and as for the society of honourable people, each one wants positive honour for himself while not being prepared to grant even negative honour to others or to allow their membership of society to go unchallenged. Each person ceaselessly threatens others' membership of this society and, if possible, strips them of it. This is the society of those who not only deprive each other of their life of honour, their civil standing, but from time to time actually take away others' natural lives. Individuals do this to each other, whole communities do it, in wars and revolutions, in religious persecution, in the persecution of heretics and witches, and in all its inchoate future forms whose names, as yet, we do not know.

Mankind's sky does not remain untroubled for long; now here, now there, the searing and crashing vilenesses of pride and hatred break out. The case of the Jews shows us a specific instance of this general situation. Things that happen only from time to time, here and there, to this or that group, are happening to Jews constantly and everywhere; it is the easiest thing to murder their honour, for it leaves no terrible external marks and can be done with impunity; physical murder is also easy, when it comes to it. That is how it must be, essentially, for the race which is cheated of its honour: in every society their membership of society is challenged, in every country people try to portray them as foreigners and insist that, living among [Ger. 'unter'] all peoples, their position should be beneath [Ger. 'unter'] all other peoples. It must be so as long as there are Jews.

It must be so for a very long time yet; for the Jews belong to every human community on account of their achievements and their human nature just like other human beings. So in the long run they cannot be excluded from any human   community,   and   are   Germans,   Englishmen, Frenchmen, etc., of Jewish descent, just as others are Germans, Englishmen, Frenchmen, etc., of other decent, whether their origins are known or unknown. And just as it is impossible, without becoming absurd, to ascribe the outstanding spiritual production of, for instance, a German of Jewish decent to anything other than German culture – to ancient Judea, perhaps, or the future Zion?! – so no German of Jewish descent, if he is thinking clearly, will dream of regarding himself as anything other than a German. His fatherland is just that: his fatherland; he feels it and gives of himself to it; all the more so since his ancestors have already given the people of his fatherland the greatest thing, the Bible, at a time when they themselves were a different people and were not his people at all. What is the most German book? The Bible in German; and it is only as the German Bible that he knows it as his Bible and his most German work of literature. Should his fatherland cease to be his fatherland because it is inhabited by people who are just as people are the world over – the same kind of human beings as the Jews, too – and because the most vile and despicable of these human beings persecute Jews and infect others, to a greater or lesser extent, with hostility towards Jews? And Jews would perpetrate the very same kind of thing against non-Jews if circumstances were different.... Hatred, indeed, utterly robs human beings of their senses, both the hated and the haters. In their hatred of Jewish Christianity and contrary to the Bible, which they expound in a diabolical manner, the anti-Semites go to the lengths of trying to wrap themselves in 'their religion', in Germanic paganism and their own virtue!

You wrap yourself in virtue tightly:
I call that being clad too lightly.

It is not the clothes that do it: what counts is the body and the heart within it. Gabriel Riessner once put it like this, with fine self-esteem: Just as Prince Lichnowski said that he considered himself no less a man of the German people because he belonged to a hitherto privileged class, he, Riessner, regarded himself in the same way in spite of belonging to a hitherto relegated class. (Gabriel Riessner was a German of Jewish descent.   In 1848 he was Vice-President of the National Assembly; he was one of its noblest men and most powerful speakers.)

The fact that the Jew Riessner belongs to Jewry as well as to the German nation no more detracts from his political, social and cultural German-ness than the fact that other Germans are Catholics, for instance, and others are philosophers, artists or mystics. The German Jew is no less German because he finds himself obliged, in response to the attacks he suffers on account of his origins, to join with other German Jews for mutual protection; this is part–a painful part–of his political and social distinctness. With their Judaism, however, the Absolute in them, right down to everything which makes them part of the relative

life of the communities, Jews belong in a significant way to the
entire life of humanity; the Jewish race is evidently something
that penetrates the whole of humanity, in time, in space, and
inwardly. Jews, for their part, with their uniquely rich world-
memory, bearing history within them in their racial memory
which goes back to the most dim and distant past, these living
human beings *are* the continuity of historical memory, and no
doubt they will not be uninvolved in the future of humanity.
The Jews are possibly the only human beings authorized and
able to furnish humanity with anything like Judaism; to that
extent they are the most interesting people in history and now
give promise of being extremely interesting. It is impossible to
arrive at a proper assessment of the significance of the Jews:
but at least for our historical epoch which, provided some
gigantic wave of world history does not sweep away everything
we know and replace it with something totally new and
fundamentally different, can rightly be called the Jewish or
Christian epoch, Jews seem to be indispensable and
irreplaceable as regards mankind's inner life. The simple
rationale for the existence of Jews is Judaism, and if there are
to be Jews, there must be anti-Semites.

Jews promote Judaism, and as we have seen anti-
Semites promote the continued existence of Jews. Provided
that antisemitism, hatred of Jews, does not cease, there will
always be Jews and Judaism. For a moment, with the shaking

of the foundations of religious superstition and the shattering of the states as confessional states, in which private law and public law were determined not only by jurisprudence but equally by the orthodox religion of the state, the hatred of Jews threatened to fade away: for a moment it seemed as though it was bound to lose its hold. But do you think the mob will ever surrender the least thing that is its own? Anyway, it cannot sing any other tune, only variations on the old melody. And the mob, once educated, simply reproduces in an educated fashion what it had before it was educated. For a long time now, instead of its uneducated religion, it has subscribed to an evolutionary monism; unfortunately this education–unlike religion–did not automatically supply hatred of Jews into the bargain. So special forms of edi-faec-ation were required to perform this task, of which the racial theory smells the strongest. One does not need a particularly sensitive nose to detect the stench, in our cultural life, of that hatred of Jews which is based on the racial theory.

Through the racial theory the hatred of Jews comes to itself once more; we must look this hatred in the eye and realize that we are entering into a new period of revitalized hatred of Jews. But this also means that the danger of Jews and Judaism becoming extinct is averted once more, for the present. Hatred of Jews lends immortality to Jews and Judaism by preventing Jews from enjoying equal rights and hence being assimilated and so disappearing. Jews are so little responsible for the hatred of Jews: in fact it is the hatred of Jews which is responsible for the Jews (not for their existence, but for their continuance). Essentially, the hatred of Jews will remain the determining factor: the actual cause remains, the catalyst remains, the combination of cause and catalyst remains. But the deeper significance remains too, and if we are to grasp the whole Jewish question we must recognize and understand this significance, in addition to realizing the basic fact that, in human affairs, we can count on nothing but men's interest, and justice must be accounted as mere babbling nonsense. (This too is babbling nonsense when, as a result of changes in the disposition of interests, those who have been hitherto at a disadvantage attain to their rights, and people speak as if justice has triumphed; for the triumph of justice is never anything else but this improvement of conditions. Why duplicate causes by saying that justice has triumphed, or even triplicate them by saying that God has produced the triumph of justice? God = justice = the improvement of conditions. Improve the conditions around you and rid yourselves of things that stand in your way, the fairy-tales and the empty words utterly lacking in objective reference, where the fairy-tales hide. Rid yourselves of the eternal ambiguity, the hovering between sense and nonsense, reality and hocus-pocus, and the confusion of one thing with another.)

The Jews as an historical means and antisemitism as the means towards this means: that is the deeper level of the issue. And in the case of the emancipation of Jews it is not a question of emancipating their honour but of emancipating their strength, which is to be rendered fruitful, once more, on the field of history. It is not a question of emancipating Jews, but of emancipating Judaism. As we have already said, history is not interested in the fact that the Jews are still without honour and are suffering at the hands of anti-Semites, no more than it is interested in the sufferings of the anti-Semites at the hands of Jews. History itself does not suffer; it does not even suffer boredom with incessant antisemitism (for, like everything else that is devoid of spirit and goes on incessantly, antisemitism ought to bore it to tears); it is only concerned that anti-semitism should do its duty in keeping the Jews alive, and that the Jews should continue to be a serviceable organ for history. Only this organ must not suffer so much that it finally stops functioning and perishes. History reacts against this; history will not allow the Jews' elemental power to be excluded from the historical process and their strength to be violated. That is emancipation, the emancipation of the Jews' strength; and the emancipation of their strength will automatically give rise, to a certain degree, to an emancipation of their honour.

People employ many remedies against antisemitism, and I can assure the reader that not one of them is of the least help; accordingly, the consolation I have just uttered will only console a few people. And only a few will be any more content when I say this: where human beings are concerned, discontentment arising *from general causes* also has its good side. The few who really count, however, who are on the right track, will find something in what I have said that can give them light and strength in their sufferings. Being a Jew, objectively speaking, means suffering injustice; for the ordinary Jew, subjectively speaking, it means fearing this injustice; but for the proper Jew, the real Israelite, it means not being afraid of it, fighting it in every possible way.[4] They will not fear this

---

[4] 'Out of the most wretched conditions, contrary to all probability, have arisen the new political and social relationships for people as a whole. Things have improved. (Only if there had not been a corresponding improvement for the Jews would they have reason to complain.) Things have improved in that the struggle has been consistently for the idea and the ideal, for what is inaccessible to view. So, instead of bemoaning what has not yet been achieved, the Jews should carry on with the struggle; they should go on fighting, always cherishing in their hearts the ideal in its entirety. They must not fight as Jews – they cannot, in any case, since they constitute no party and are not joined together in any organization. They should fight the way the Persians prayed: no Persian, at the sacrifices, was supposed to ask the gods for himself alone; he was always to pray for the whole community. Committing themselves to history, let the Germans of Jewish descent be first among Germans to fight for the genuine unity of Germany and for its genuine freedom, and lend their strength to the national movement towards realizing a state characterized by justice and freedom. "If with one hand you were to offer me emancipation, the goal of all my most heartfelt desires, and with the other the realization of the beautiful dream of Germany's political unity, linked with its political freedom, without any further consideration I would choose the latter! For I have the firm and profound conviction that it contains and implies the former." So spoke Gabriel Riessner in 1835, and these noble, powerful and true words which then referred to the obtaining of emancipation, still apply today and henceforward with regard to its implementation.' (*Der Judenhass und die Juden*, pp. 281, 282, 3rd para.)

injustice too much, and will fight against it, yet without cherishing the hope that it will be entirely vanquished and that they could ever succeed in bringing their honour as perceived by the world in line with their worth and the contribution they make.   True Israelites, however, also think differently from ordinary Jews with regard to the honour they might receive from the world; they think differently from ordinary society about its norms of prestige, according to which the human being and his achievement are not valued in terms of value, but only in terms of prestige.   True Israelites do not have a high opinion of the honour this world apportions or denies, for the world has never shown itself capable of distinguishing the greatest geniuses from the greatest criminals.   Instead of giving positive honour to its holiest sons (for it has nothing else to give them), it has preferred to take away their negative honour and has actually *punished* the noblest virtue and manifestations of spirit, as if they were vices practised by its very scum; the world has punished its saints with curses, with all the filth of its repugnance, with death by torture and the desecration of their corpses.   True Israelites will not have a high estimate of the honour that is apportioned or denied by such a non-thinking society, which thinks of nothing but its own interest and pursues it with such obtuseness, crudity, insolence and villainy; it takes anything it can by freebooting, and where it gives honour, it does so hypocritically – how, generally speaking, do those who give honour view those to whom they give it!

In contrast to the way it honours people, this society is quite serious when it comes to despising, insulting and slandering people. And where Jews are concerned, in their special situation, honour in ordinary society never has a straightforward meaning, not even in the sense of customary social practice; for, as we know, not only is the Jew not held to be worth what he and his achievement are really worth, but the value of his achievement is not even attributed to him; in fact, in society at large, he remains exposed to more or less successful swindling and violation. Consequently all Jews are obliged to say, like base characters and geniuses, 'We do not ask about honour or disgrace!'; they are obliged to despise their being despised (*spernere te sperni!*) – it does not touch them; it is like a bird, a swallow flying off. Jews must always be ready to accept the fact that they will be cheated of their rights by a deceitful society. Rudolf von Ihering is correct on this *one* point when he writes: 'The monstrous tragedy of Shylock's fate does not lie in his being denied what is his right, but in the fact that he, a Jew in the middle ages, *believes in this right,* – as it were, *just as if he were a Christian!* He has a rocklike, imperturbable belief in justice, which the Judge himself encourages, until, like a thunderbolt, the catastrophe bursts upon him, wrenching him from his delusion and making it plain to him that he is nothing but the outlawed Jew of the middle ages who is *given* justice by being *cheated* of it.'

All Jews ought really to be thinking people. If Jews are special in the world, in every way, they should take heart and press forward, completely resolute and determined; they should be prepared at least to think in a special way, which means nothing other than to reflect upon the special thing that they are, namely, Jews. They need to get out of this vacillating state of mind in which some are trapped by the idea of a future assimilation, and others are trapped by the idea of a future Zionism. What they need is to be able resolutely to think through what is special to themselves, their own destiny, the fact that they are Jews; nothing more is necessary. Nor does this mean that Jews need to have a particular programme. No programme, no dreams, no 'principle' or 'spirit' of Judaism; they do not even need to know what the 'cause' of Judaism is. All they need is to look quite practically and see what actually is Jewish in the world, what Jewish elements there have been in the world so far. They only need to make a proper start to grasp what it means, to come to grips with it, having no regard to the narrowness of their prejudices up to now; they only need to conduct themselves honestly and bravely as those who possess, use and administer what is distinctively Jewish, and above all they must take Christ unto themselves (see the address, *'Wir wollen ihn züruck!'* (*Der Judenhass und die Juden* Chapter VIII, *cf.* bibliography). If they know what is Jewish in the world, they will immediately know more of what they are as Jews, and of Judaism. For what can a Jew know about Judaism if he does not know that Christianity is Jewish? In any case, what are these things, 'spirit,' 'principle' and 'cause'? The spirit and principle of Judaism is something hidden within them, in the Jews (history will find it out!), and the fact that they are Jews, that is their cause, by which they stand firm, however near to the centre or far from it the individual may stand. This is their good cause, even without any programme; they *do* their programme, which is a mystery even to themselves since it is not they who do it. Thus they do, actualize themselves and somehow or other carry fire among mankind. They should know and believe, regarding both the known that has been and the unknown that is to come, that they have done this, that it will continue to need doing, and that they will do it, if only they do not neglect what is specific to them, if only they allow *their higher life* to exercise its influence. To believe and know this is their profession of faith and their initiation into Judaism and being Jewish. And indeed, there has never been a lack of right action, of action in response to the right and great word, on the part of Jews; even today *their* powerful word and their river of song is in the world, constantly self-renewing action. But as for words which are not deeds, as for looking for words before deeds and needing programmes for historical action – how pitiful! That is something they should not ask for, that is the worst kind of Jewish question. They can and must be Jews without having a programme, for they are the mysteriously elemental constituent of nature's being, its unfolding and fulfillment; they are the world's one element – an element that is as great as the world and puts forth its power through the whole world. They are Jews, whose fire is fitting for the world, and thus it is fitting for them to be Jews. They should reflect upon the fact that they are Jews and, pondering their origins in the past and the future that is in store for them, take account not only of the lowly, but also of the lofty aspects of their calling. They should remember that, like the most Jewish of Jews, of whom it is written that he was hated without a cause like no one else on earth, they exist both in the state of humiliation and in the state of exaltation, *ignominia hominis* and *gloria hominis*. Taking up the world's challenge and returning it, they could clothe themselves with honour on the basis of their sublime fullness, like Christ; they could turn their disgrace into an honour and wear it like a crown, just as Christ, in uttermost humiliation, calls himself a king.

Yes: if only Jews would *think*! No people in the world find themselves directed towards thinking as much as the Jews do; for in their own bodies they experience the truth that human beings are non-thinking, respectable in delivering blows but miserable in delivering judgments. No other people have such concrete reasons for thinking, on account of their life and the relationship of their race to mankind and mankind's history. If Jews were to think, they would experience a tremendous increase in morale, security and fighting power; but only if they would think. Jews are eternally at war with terrible enemies; but, equipped with real thought and the awareness of their historical distinctiveness and their continuing spiritual task, they will be able to dwell in a strong, impregnable citadel. Provided they think, they will not lose much by being deprived of their honour (which is not the result of misdeeds and omissions on their part); particularly if, like thinkers, they recall that there is honourable disgrace as well as shameful disgrace, and if, again like thinkers, they refuse to attach any absolute value to honour. Instead, those who think – not attributing absolute value to either honour, possessions, or love, i.e., not to life either, to this sack of flesh and blood, not even when they are able to live in their sack with the freedom which comes from possessing all honours – instead, those who are transformed in their lives by the spirit and, in spite of being intertwined with life in the most important ways, are elevated above it, find their consolation in what is genuinely Absolute, even where their lives are characterized by unfreedom and inhibition: they are saved. In thought, the gate of freedom is opened wide to them; they have profoundly forgotten honour and have become too big for it.

Yes, if the Jews were to *think*, it would be the key to their prison. (At a single stroke everything would be different in their own eyes, including their interest and the way they view what happens to them, happiness or ill-fortune.) Yes, if people were to think like thinking human beings – not merely as they do now, with their immature ideas of things and names, *but think of that which has no name* and is not a thing – then the Jews would no longer need to think in their special way at all! But there is no point in thinking that men will ever think. Any one who *thinks*, or who thinks at least now and again, or even who is not terribly interested in 'thinking' in the way people 'think', finds it simply incredible *that human beings think as they do and form such judgments about their own kind*! If they knew what thinking and judging really means, they would not believe themselves able to do it, and they would give up all hope of ever learning how. 'It is inconceivable that reason should ever become popular,' writes Goethe; 'passions and feelings may become popular, but reason will always be in the possession of only a few outstanding men.... For the most part, the world consists only of ill-will and envy.'

Men do not think and cannot by any means be brought to think. This is plain in the case of the Jews: in spite of having a wealth of stimuli, they do not think, no more than they have ever done, but are stuck in the merely earthly interest of blind egoism. And so, earthly men that they are, they will continue to experience severe attacks on account of their lack of honour in an unholy and oppressed life. It is this that drives them to fight for their honour and their right, the highest right a human being can enjoy in society, namely, the right to live as an honourable and free man. And this is the one thing: they seem to be weak vis-à-vis the world, although they defend themselves against those who murder their honour and freedom as any man would defend himself against a murderer. But the murderers are stronger and unscrupulous. All the same, if someone strikes them, they should strike back, and if there are too many attacking them, they must stake their lives on their freedom – for the animal is prepared to pay the price of life itself for its freedom. And if anyone has never been struck himself, let him strike the man who has struck his brother. We have learned this from both Jews and human beings, and so did our great Moses, Mosheh rabbenu, the great teacher of Jews and of mankind.

The other thing is this: they remain Jews. And since this cannot come about through their reflecting on their historical and spiritual reality, profoundly at one with themselves, it comes about through the fictions of self-deception. So it was in earlier times, when they had far less idea as to their significance for the world in which they lived; then too, superstition was their support, enabling everything in them to offer resistance to the whole world and giving them a belief in themselves – in a life, lacking all beauty, all music, at a time of such misery, when they were under the most terrible of curses, the curse of having no fatherland! There was still something broad and remote, and a certain radiance, about all their misery and their superstitious hoping; this was the breadth and remoteness of history and the radiance of Judaism, whose true soul is always clear, however confused and superstitious the Jews may be....

The Jews wanted to go out into the world with their Judaism. Thus the Jews, while they were still a nation, were the only nation to think about all the other nations, about the future of mankind and the human species. For no animal thinks about its own species, and among men it was the Jews who first thought about the human species. Zion was only the preparatory stage for Jews and Judaism in the world: 'It is a light thing that thou shouldest be my servant to raise up the tribes of Jacob, and to restore the preserved of Israel: I will also give thee for a light to the Gentiles, that thou mayest be my salvation unto the end of the earth' (Isa. 49:6). Jews and Judaism belong within history and within the world, even if it contained a hundred times more anti-Semites.

Zion is of no consequence,[*] no more than heaven (and no Jews, assuredly, will get to heaven), but Jews in the world are and remain of consequence. The world needs the Jews. If it had no Jews, it would quickly notice and become aware of the lack – not, of course, in the cognizant way, with concepts and thoughts, but in the way the stomach knows when it is hungry and thirsty. Now that the Jews are in the world, however, all those who have the ability to know, should cultivate a proper and intellectual knowledge of the Jews' presence in the world as something that is and remains important, in spite of all the world's murderers who would like

---

[*] with regard to the hatred of Jews. Zion has, however, given the Jews their highest emancipation: a state and corresponding nationhood, has raised prestige and honour of the Jews in the world through Israel's military, technological, agricultural and cultural achievements. (The Editor)

to get hold of them, their blood-murderers; and in spite of those other murderers, those who kill the inner personality, honour, who plan civil murder for them, together with the hell of being civilly dead. The Jews are stronger than this death and hell together; they are a strong something that renders the earth's soil fruitful; they are a major, primal, creative power in human history; and the anti-Semites' task is an endless one. Jews must abandon all hope of annihilating antisemitism, for that, as we have seen, would signify their own death: it would be the Jews' natural death, and they would dissolve and perish in the world's justice, if *Memsheleth sadon, the realm of pride,* came to an end in the utter bliss of a growth of justice and love. But the world is and remains unjust, so its injustice towards Jews remains and the Jew-haters and anti-Semites remain. And they, in turn, will not succeed, with all their yelling, spitting, biting and tearing, in wiping out the life-force which animates the Jews. For the stronger the hatred of Jews is, the stronger the Jews become. Hence the only counsel of any use to the diligent Jew-haters is that which the Koran gives to the enemies of Muhammad: 'If anyone is angered because Muhammad cannot be brought down, let him hang himself from the first rafter of his house, and he will soon feel his anger abating.'

The Jews will not die, but live. Again: antisemitism keeps Judaism alive, it keeps the Jews Jews; all it does is show them the extent of the hostility, the risk and the dangers which confront them, corresponding to their importance. Seen in the context of history, as a mere stimulus to Judaism, antisemitism loses all its opposition and enmity towards it: *discordia concors*. Antisemitism belongs to the class of indispensable historical means, like wars, whereby honourable men become murderers and criminals and call themselves heroes. And the heroism of antisemitism seems genuinely understandable in this human race, in which war never ceases anywhere, because it is ruled by egoism and the moralistic criticism which is not the physician of egoism, but its disease; because it is ruled by egoistic interest with its infinite rights and the demon of pride – Satan is the prince of this world, walking about like a roaring lion. Consequently those who preach justice, holiness, brotherhood, and love among men – this utterly stupid teaching, which we have all heard – are bound to cut ridiculous and despicable figures. Who has spoken of these things with the greatest earnestness, who has made these superfluous words the most beautiful and self-evident in the world, and who has placed justice at least at the world's end? Jews. Surely it is quite right, accordingly, that the world should relegate the Jews to the very tail end of justice, and attribute the pride and hatred unleashed against them simply to 'the damned Jews' themselves? Surely it is right for the world to call them 'damned Jews' in the same breath as it speaks of revolution, war, famine and plague; and should they not have the greatest derision, shame and misery heaped on their necks, and be regarded as furthest removed from brotherhood, love, justice and holiness, as if they were not human beings at all?

No. They are still being treated unjustly. This must be said, although there is no justice on earth, and this matter cannot be adjudged and will perhaps never be put right. Just as the Jews do not resemble the prototype of man they themselves have drawn up, neither do they resemble antisemitism's distorted image. In all truth, they are not the cause of the hatred which is continually surging around them, and they can say: You do not know us. You do not know us; it is only pride that says we are not human beings like you. We are not told this by those who do not treat us with pride, nor by the animals (who show no pride at all), nor by the trees, the grasses and flowers, the mountains, rivers and oceans; the stars do not speak like this; nature has made us human beings, and as such we have to assert ourselves against countless enemies. We are human beings; we are human beings who are of significance for mankind. It may be that our teaching on justice, holiness, brotherhood and love does not suit mankind – the Jewish teaching of the advance of history does not suit mankind; the *nature* of mankind will not permit such a *history: the world will not admit the Spirit*! All the same, driven as we are, we have been compelled to proclaim the *Spirit* and testify that it is no empty word, but a reality, higher than the world, the only genuine reality and bliss, and the invisible foundation on which mankind rests, without knowing it.

While we have not been able to move men to embrace the *Spirit*, we *have* moved them, and no one else can stand up and claim to have achieved so much for mankind.   With the strength of a tempest, we have achieved the greatest thing possible: and now we must and will say this of ourselves – contrary to what you say of us! And in doing so, we are uttering the pure truth; history confirms it. History does not listen to the anti-Semites, and of the Jews it says this: 'Harsh mother that I am, I rejoice in their strength; and I rejoice in their prophets, with their defiance that comes from their strength, who arise like a storm that comes from the sea, terrifying the land so that it imagines it will be swept hence like the raging waters.' History says: 'I cause everyone to do what he can – the anti-Semites make wind, but the Jews create a tempest.'

BIBLIOGRAPHY

Works by Constantin Brunner

Die Lehre von den Geistigen und vom Volke. Berlin: Schnabel, 1908; 2d ed. Potsdam: Kiepenheuer, 1927; 3d ed. Stuttgart: Cotta, 1962.

Spinoza gegen Kant und die Sache der geistigen Wahrheit. Berlin: Schnabel, 1910.

Der Judenhass und die Juden. Berlin: Oesterheld & Co., 1918; 3d ed. 1919.

Memscheleth Sadon. Letztes Wort über den Judenhass und die Juden. Berlin: Verlag Neues Vaterland, 1920.

Unser Christus oder das Wesen des Genies. Berlin: Oesterheld & Co., 1921; 2d ed. Cologne: Kiepenheuer-Witsch, 1958.

Der Judenhass und das Denken. Berlin: Philo-Verlag, 1922.

Liebe, Ehe, Mann und Weib. Potsdam: Kiepenheuer, 1924; 2d ed. Stuttgart: Cotta, 1965.

Vom Einsiedler Constantin Brunner. Potsdam: Kiepenheuer, 1924.

Aberglaube an die Ärzte und an die Heilmittel. Potsdam: Kiepenheuer, 1927.

Aus meinem Tagebuch. Potsdam: Kiepenheuer, 1928; 2d ed. Stuttgart: Cotta, 1967.

Materialismus und Idealismus. Potsdam: Kiepenheuer, 1928; 2d ed. Cologne: Kiepenheuer-Witsch, 1959.

Natura sanat, medicus curat. Stuttgart: Hippokrates Verlag, 1928.

Von den Pflichten der Juden und von den Pflichten des Staates. Berlin: Kiepenheuer, 1930.

Höre Israel und Höre Nicht-Israel (Die Hexen). Berlin: Kiepenheuer, 1931.

Posthumous Works by Constantin Brunner

Unser Charkter oder Ich bin der Richtige! Zürich: Humanitas Verlag, 1939; 2d ed. (including *Geburtstagsbrief and Kurze Rechenschaft*) Stuttgart: Cotta, 1964.

Kunst, Philosophie, Mystik (Gesammelte Aufsätze). Zürich: Humanitas Verlag, 1940.

Der entlarvte Mensch. Den Haag: Nijhoff, 1951.

Vermächtnis. Den Haag, 1952.

Translations

Bekius, Evert: *Constantin Brunner: Het fiktieve Denken*; Van Gorcum, Assen 1984.

Bermann, Aron: *Ha-filosofia Schel Constantin Brunner*; Tel Aviv 1957.

Bernard, Walter: *The Unity of Body and Mind* (L. Bickel: Innen und Aussen); Philosophical Library Inc., N. Y. 1959.

Lurié, Henri: *Constantin Brunner: Spinoza contre Kant et la cause de la Véritié spirituelle*; Paris 1932.

Rappaport, Aron. M.: *Constantin Brunner: Our Christ, The Revolt of the Mystical Genius*; Van Gorcum & Co., Assen 1990.

Schneider, Mira: *Constantin Brunner: Materialismo E Idalismo*; Buenos Aires 1961; 2d ed. 1970.

Sonntag, Leo: *Constantin Brunner - L'Amour*; Paris 1967. *Constantin Brunner, 'un philosophe hors les murs'* in: *Cahiers du Sud*, Vol. 51, No. 375, 1964.

Suhl, Abraham and Bernard, Walter: *Science, Spirit, Superstition - A new Enquiry into Human Thought*; Allan & Unwin, University of Toronto Press, London & Toronto, 1968.

187

Excerpts from Pertaining Literature

Baraz, Michael: *La révolution inésperée, Constantin Brunner*; Corti, Paris 1986.

Bernard, Walter: *The Philosophy of Spinoza and Brunner*; Spinoza Institute of America, N.Y. 1934.

Bickel, Lothar: *Zur Renaissance der Philosophie*; Kiepenheuer, Berlin 1931;

–2. *Auflage mit Studien zu einigen Dialogen Platons*; Diana, Zürich 1975.

–*Nachruf: Constantin Brunner 1862-1937*; Philosophia 1937.

–*Wirklichkeit und Wahrheit des Denkens*; Diana, Zürich/Stuttgart 1953.

Brunner, Lotte: *Es gibt kein Ende...Die Tagebücher*; ed. L. Sonntag & H. Stolte, Hansa, Hamburg 1970.

Eisenstein, Israel: *'Die Philosophie Constantin Brunners'* in: *Archiv für die Geschichte der Philosophie* Bd. 53; 1971.

–'Ist die Evolutionstheorie wissenschaflich begründet? Das Artproblem in biologischer und philosphischer Sicht,' in: *Philosophia Naturalis* Bd. 15; 1975.

Eisenstein, I. und Grünberg Ph.: *Auf den Pfaden der Philosophie Spinozas und Constantin Brunners*, ed. L. Sonntag & H. Stolte; Anton Hain, Königstein/Ts 1982.

Goetz, George: *Philosophie und Judentum*; Hansa Verlag, Husum 1991.

Goetz, Hans: *Leben ist Denken -- Eine Schrift zur Renaissance der Philosophie des deutschen Denkers Constantin Brunner*; Athenäum Verlag, Frankfurt a/M 1987.

Grünberg, Phöbus: Der Begriff Philosophie in der Lehre Constantin Brunners; ICBI, HAAG 1985.

Sonntag, Leo: 'Constantin Brunner' in: *Temps modernes*, 1, 1952.

Sterian, Moshe: Einführung in das Ideenreich Spinozas. Diana, Zürich 1972.

188

Stolte, Heinz: *Vom Feuer der Wahrheit -- Der Philosoph Constantin Brunner*; Hansa, Hamburg 1968. 3.erweiterte Aufl. Hansa, Hamburg 1990.

–Israel, Eisenstein: *Ein neuer Beitrag zum Verständnis Spinozas*; Athenäum, Frankfurt 1989.

INDEX

Dr Heinz Briske
(Victim of the Holocaust)

FROM A LETTER TO THE EDITOR BY SIR JEHUDI MENUHIN,
AN ADMIRER OF C. BRUNNER
AND FOLLOWER OF HIS PHILOSOPHY:

'The Jew is conditioned by the relentless fate of hatred. He will survive the religious, racial, political and economic attempts of annihilation with a high content of spiritual baggage, of intellectual acuity, of sense of destiny, though packed in battered and bloodied suitcases, to carry his message of hope and despair beyond the numbered days of other peoples.'